ROOT-CAUSE THERAPY

A Method for True, Lasting Change

Melissa Hiemann

Co-Founder, The Centre for Healing

Root-Cause Therapy: A Method for True, Lasting Change

First published 2026

Published by The Centre for Healing

thecentreforhealing.com

Important Notice and Disclaimer

This book is intended for educational and informational purposes only. The content presented here is not a substitute for professional psychological, psychiatric, medical, or clinical advice, diagnosis, or treatment. Nothing in this book constitutes clinical training, and reading this book does not qualify, certify, or license any person to practise Root-Cause Therapy, psychotherapy, counselling, or any other regulated health profession.

Root-Cause Therapy (RCT) is a complementary and alternative modality. Practitioners wishing to offer RCT professionally must complete the full RCT certification programme through The Centre for Healing. Certification, accreditation requirements, and scope of practice information are available at thecentreforhealing.com.

The case studies and client examples presented in this book are drawn from real clinical work. Names and identifying details have been changed or composited to protect client confidentiality. Any resemblance to specific individuals is coincidental.

The author and publisher make no representations or warranties of any kind, express or implied, about the completeness, accuracy, or suitability of the information contained in this book for any particular purpose. The author and publisher disclaim all liability for any loss, injury, or damage arising directly or indirectly from the use or reliance on the information presented.

Readers experiencing mental health difficulties, trauma, addiction, or any other health concerns are encouraged to seek support from a qualified health professional.

ISBN: 978-0-6489460-2-1

Printed at a facility closest to you to reduce the environmental impact.

TCFH™

About the Author

Melissa Hiemann is a trauma-informed healer, certified practitioner trainer, and co-founder of The Centre for Healing, a globally recognised training organisation dedicated to bringing effective trauma healing to practitioners and clients worldwide.

Melissa's journey into healing began not in a classroom but in her own life. After years of navigating the aftermath of childhood trauma, domestic violence, and the patterns that followed, she found her way to transformative healing work in her mid-twenties. What changed everything was not advice or coping tools — it was the discovery of root-cause approaches that reached beneath the surface of symptoms to address the experiences and beliefs that had been quietly driving her patterns all along.

In 2014, Melissa became a certified coach. Almost immediately, she recognised that something was still missing from conventional Neuro-Linguistic Programming (NLP) and coaching frameworks. She began weaving together a richer tapestry of approaches — shamanic practices, somatic processes, breathwork, inner child healing, reparenting, and family constellations — searching for the combination that could produce lasting change rather than temporary relief. What emerged from that search became the foundation of Root-Cause Therapy.

In 2016, Melissa co-founded The Centre for Healing with her partner Ryan Hassan. For nearly five years, they ran a completely booked-out alternative mental health and addiction clinic — a team-based practice offering an integrative, root-cause approach where conventional treatment had repeatedly fallen short. Working with hundreds of clients across anxiety, depression, trauma, addiction, and relationship patterns, they witnessed again and again what the mainstream system had rarely managed to achieve: not symptom management, but lasting resolution.

In 2021, Melissa and Ryan began training other practitioners. Since then, The Centre for Healing has certified practitioners across the world — coaches, therapists, counsellors, nurses, social workers, and people with no prior clinical background who simply knew, from their own experience, that this work needed to exist in the world. Many of the original clients became practitioners themselves, now running full-time healing practices of their own.

As The Centre for Healing approaches its tenth year, this book is offered as both a resource and a celebration of the method, the community, the students who believed in the vision, and the possibility of a world in which trauma stops being passed from generation to generation.

Melissa is also the author of The Natural High — Secrets to Overcoming Instant Gratification and Finding Inner Peace, a companion text exploring the emotional and neurological foundations of compulsive behaviour and the path to genuine inner regulation.

Acknowledgements

This book would not exist without the extraordinary community that has grown around The Centre for Healing over the past decade.

To Ryan Hassan, my partner, co-founder, and the person who has walked every step of this journey with me. You believed in this vision when it was still just a question we were asking together. You held the space when the work got hard, pushed back when it needed it, and have been the most steadfast presence in everything we have built. This is as much yours as it is mine.

To our long-term students, the ones who found us early, trusted the process before there was a track record to point to, and went on to build practices and lives that demonstrate every day what this work makes possible. Watching you grow has been one of the great privileges of our professional lives. As we approach ten years, we celebrate every one of you.

To our original clients, particularly those who came to the outpatient clinic in those first years, when we were still learning the full shape of what this method could do. You trusted us with your most tender material. Many of you are now practitioners yourselves, carrying this work into the world in your own unique way. That means everything.

To our families and friends who believed in us, who listened to us talk about trauma and nervous systems and unconscious minds at dinner tables and on long walks and in the middle of ordinary days, who supported us through the uncertainty of building something new, and who never once suggested we should try something safer. We felt your belief, and it mattered more than you know.

And to everyone reading this book, whether you are a practitioner in training, someone who has experienced this work and wants to understand it more deeply, or someone who simply felt called by the title. You are welcome here. The work is for you.

How to Use This Book

Root-Cause Therapy: A Method for True, Lasting Change is written for anyone who wants to understand this method deeply, whether you are considering certification, currently in training, or an established practitioner looking to deepen your practice.

The book moves through six parts: the foundational philosophy, the science, the method, specialised protocols, personal stories, and practical guidance for building your practice. You can read it from cover to cover or move directly to the sections most relevant to where you are.

Connect With The Centre for Healing

Follow us on Social media and tag us for a shoutout with a photo of this book: @thecentreforhealing

Explore courses, blogs, free resources, app and podcast, and join our community: thecentreforhealing.com

PART ONE

The Problem With Surface Level Healing

PART ONE — THE PROBLEM WITH SURFACE LEVEL HEALING

Chapter One: My Defining Moment

Before the understanding came the living of it. This is a story of lived experience.

The coping mechanisms arrived early. By fourteen, my mother had left a domestic violence situation, moving herself and two very young children out of danger while I navigated the aftermath as a young teenager — not yet equipped to process what I had witnessed and experienced, not yet knowing that processing was even something that needed to happen. No one told me that emotions didn't just disappear because you stopped looking at them. No one told me they went somewhere — into the body, into the nervous system, into the decisions you would make for decades without knowing why. No one asked me how I was; there was no emotional maturity. Not only that, my father's home didn't feel safe either. My stepmother was a narcissist. I also was bullied and alone at primary school. So, nowhere and no one really felt safe.

So I found other ways to feel okay. When you discover something that offers you a sense of peace, ease, or confidence, especially when accessing those states on your own feels impossible, the brain burns it in as a signal. It becomes a memory, a pathway, a pull. I was drawn to the wrong crowd not from a lack of character but from a deep sense that I belonged with the ones who also felt like outcasts. We recognised each other. And in that recognition, for a while, was something that felt like relief.

The substances came later, but the pattern underneath them was already there: I was trying to feel okay. We all are. Every coping mechanism, every compulsion, every seemingly self-destructive behaviour — at its root, it is a human being trying to find their way back to a feeling of safety that was taken from them before they even knew how to ask for it. I did not understand this at fourteen. I would not fully understand it until I was twenty-seven and sitting across from a person who would change the course of my life.

But here is what I want to tell you about those years, because I think it matters deeply for the work we are doing in this book. Even in the middle of all of it, the substances, the toxic relationships, the self-sabotage, the coping and the numbing and the circling — there was something else. A flame. Small, but persistent. Something deep inside me that I could not explain and could not extinguish, no matter how hard I tried, no matter how much evidence accumulated around me that I was not capable of more.

I saw people living differently. People who could speak their truth, build something, lead, love well, make an impact. I was so inspired by them. And underneath that inspiration was a grief I didn't have words for, a grief that whispered: maybe that could never be me.

I didn't know then that this grief was not a verdict. It was a wound. And wounds, unlike verdicts, can heal.

My first real awakening came not through a dramatic revelation but through a quiet act of courage. I admitted — to myself, for the first time, that my patterns were not just bad luck. That I was not simply a victim of circumstance, though circumstances had certainly played their part. I became vulnerable enough to seek help. And in doing so, I experienced what I now recognise as the first shift of consciousness that root-cause work creates: the realisation that we are not just living in the present moment. We are living in our past and our future simultaneously, driven by forces we cannot see until someone helps us look.

It was an old friend who mentioned a mutual contact who had become some kind of life coach. I hesitated. I had a memory of sitting in a school counsellor's office as a teenager — one cry for help, met with silence and careful listening and nothing more. I understood later why active listening has its place. But that day, what I needed was not just to be heard. I needed to be seen. And the difference between those two things is, I would come to learn, the entire difference between therapy that manages and therapy that transforms.

I connected with the coach and booked a session. What happened in that room woke something in me that I had not known was sleeping. I was introduced, for the first time, to the idea that my past was not simply behind me — it was inside me, running the show. That the relationships I kept finding myself in, the losses that kept repeating, the patterns I couldn't seem to break, no matter how much I wanted to — these were not evidence of a flawed character. They were evidence of unprocessed experiences. Of emotions that had never been allowed to complete their journey through the body.

I walked out of that session feeling something I had never felt before. Not fixed. Not advised. Awakened. As though someone had opened a window in a room I had been living in with the curtains permanently drawn. Colours were actually brighter, and I felt a love and connection to the world like I had never experienced before.

Not long afterwards, I eagerly enrolled in my first training in Neuro-Linguistic Programming (NLP) and Hypnotherapy. I remember sitting in the room during one of the early sessions when something shifted in my chest, what felt like a lightening bolt from my soul, a recognition so strong it felt physical. This. This is what I am meant to be doing. A burning sense of purpose, arriving all at once, the kind that doesn't ask for permission or wait for you to feel ready.

Everything changed immediately. Not because my past disappeared — it didn't. But because I finally had a container for it. A framework for understanding why I was the way I was, and, more importantly, that I did not have to remain that way. Neurological pathways could change. Beliefs could be updated. Emotions that had been locked inside the body for decades could be released. I was not sentenced to repeat the patterns of my upbringing. I was simply, until that moment, without the tools to do anything else.

What I had not anticipated was what the healing would do to my capacity in other areas of my life. I had struggled through school — genuinely struggled, not just found it uninteresting. I had effectively failed Year Nine and Year Ten. I could not concentrate. I found studying close to impossible, and had quietly filed away an assumption that this was simply who I was, that my brain did not work that way, that academic and intellectual pursuits were for other people. What I discovered as the healing progressed was that this was not a fact about my mind. It was a symptom. So much of my energy — the finite charge of attention and cognitive capacity that should have been available for learning, for focus, for presence in the classroom — had been held hostage in the unresolved. Spread across every fragment of trauma that had never been completed, every emotional bubble still waiting for its moment, every piece of the past that was still running as though it were happening now. As those fragments healed, that energy returned. My memory improved dramatically. I could concentrate, study, retain information in ways I had never been able to before. I was not a different person. I was the same person, but now actually present — rather than partly absent, partly still in the past, partly bracing for the future.

As I continued to study, I began to encounter knowledge that built upon knowledge. I discovered the work of Dr. David Hawkins and his[6] exploration of the energy of emotions — how the frequency of what we carry in our bodies dictates our capacity to access higher states without the crutch of addictive behaviour. I began to see my own addictions not as moral failures but as emotional substitutes, a self-medication, filling in for the peace and connection I did not yet know how to generate from within. As this understanding deepened, the compulsions began to loosen. Not all at once. Not without effort. But with a consistency I had never experienced from willpower alone, because this time, I was working at the root.

What I was building, slowly and through years of study and practice and my own healing, was a methodology. I had pieced together approaches from many traditions — Neuro-Linguistic Programming (NLP), hypnotherapy, somatic work, breathwork, inner child healing, regression, gestalt, family constellations — and refined them through thousands of sessions into something that had its own coherent shape. For a long time I thought of it as emotional healing therapy, or emotions-focused therapy, because what the work was really doing, at its heart, was helping people complete the emotional processes that had been interrupted. It was Ryan — my partner, my collaborator, the person who saw the work from the outside with fresh eyes — who said it most clearly: this is root cause therapy. That is what it does. It goes to the root. Everything else follows from there. And the name, once named, felt true in a way that the alternatives hadn't quite managed. Because that is exactly what this work is. Not symptom management. Not coping skill development. Not reframing or restructuring or learning to think differently. Going to the root. And healing it there.

— — —

I share all of this not because I believe a healer must have lived through suffering to be of service — though I do believe lived experience brings a particular quality of presence and embodiment to this work. I share it because I want you to understand, from the very first pages of this book, what Root-Cause Therapy is actually doing. It is not teaching people to think differently about their pain. It is helping them finish the emotional processes that were interrupted — sometimes decades ago, sometimes before they had words — so that the nervous system can finally release what it has been guarding, and the person can return to themselves.

I have seen this happen in people who came to me after years of talk therapy, still circling the same wound. I have seen it happen in a single session with a client who had carried a belief for 40 years and released it in 40 minutes once we found the root cause. I have seen it happen in practitioners who trained with me and then watched it unfold in their own clients — not because of exceptional talent, but because they had learned how to ask the right question at the right moment, and how to hold the space for what followed. I feel blessed to get positive comments almost daily about how it's changed practitioners' lives and their clients'.

The flame that kept burning in me through all of those difficult years — I believe now that it was not stubbornness or blind optimism. It was my soul's knowing that there was a way through. That the life I could sense on the other side of all that pain was not a fantasy but a destination. That it was, in fact, never too late.

A dear friend once said something to me that I have carried ever since, and that I return to whenever I sit with a client who has begun to grieve the childhood they never had.

> *"It is never too late to have a good childhood."*

These words gave me hope when hope felt unreasonable. They have given hope to many of the people who have sat across from me in sessions. And they are, in essence, the promise at the heart of Root-Cause Therapy, that no matter what has happened, no matter how long ago, no matter how deeply it was buried or how many layers have accumulated on top of it, healing is available. The original self, the one who existed before the conditioning and the coping and the survival strategies took hold, is still there. Still whole. Still waiting. Ready to evolve with the wisdom that you've gained through the pain.

We are simply going to help people find their way back to it. To remember their true essence and what they are really capable of in this life.

That is what this work is. That is what this book is about. And that is where we begin.

Take a moment to reflect: was there a point in your life when you first began to sense that something underneath the surface needed attention — a quiet knowing that healing was possible or needed?

Your reflection:

— — —

Chapter Two: What Healing Was Missing

I built a lot of walls. Not deliberately. Not consciously. I never allowed anyone to get truly close, because closeness had never felt safe. I moved through my teenage years accumulating layers of ego, a kind of armour that told me I was fine, that being a rebel was a choice rather than a response, that I didn't need what I was quietly desperate for. The acting out put me in risky situations. The trauma compounded. And underneath it all, buried beneath the performance of not caring, a child was still sitting with emotions she had never been taught to process and nowhere to put them.

I was in high school when I first tried to ask for help. I walked into the counsellor's office carrying something I did not have the words for, a weight of accumulated experience that had been pressing on me for years, and I shared a little of what was happening. The risky behaviour. The edges I was walking. A small window into a life that needed someone to see it clearly and respond.

What I received was listening.

I want to be careful here, because I know that active listening is valuable. Holding space is a genuinely important skill, and I have spent years learning how to do it well. But that day, as a teenager sitting across from a counsellor with one small cry for help, what I needed was not simply to be heard. I needed someone to notice. To ask the right questions. To look at the picture I was describing and gently, carefully look behind it — to wonder aloud about what might be happening at home, to flag what they were seeing, to do something with what I had offered.

Nothing came back. No questions. No concern raised. No red flags acknowledged. Just listening, and then the session ended.

I walked out and quietly closed the door on therapy. If that was what it was — someone sitting with you while you circled your pain without ever getting closer to the centre of it — then I did not see the point. I would manage on my own. I was, as it turned out, already very good at that. Managing. Surviving. Keeping the weight distributed so that no single part of me collapsed under it entirely.

It would be another decade before I tried again.

— — —

The years between that counsellor's office and my late twenties were years of pattern. Financial gains and losses that cycled with a regularity I couldn't explain. Relationships that followed the same patterns, no matter how different the person. A persistent need for the approval of men that I recognised but could not seem to stop acting from. Substances to soften the edges of emotions I had never learned to move through. A creeping awareness that my life was not going the way I wanted it to, coupled with a helplessness about what to do because every time I tried to change the behaviour without understanding what was underneath it, the change didn't last. The willpower ran out. The pattern reasserted itself. And I returned to the familiar territory of wondering whether this was simply who I was.

The breakthrough, when it finally came, arrived through a conversation rather than a crisis. I was confiding in an old friend about a recent heartbreak — another relationship that had ended in the same way the ones before it had ended, when he mentioned that a mutual friend had become some kind of life coach. Something in me responded before my mind had time to talk it out of it. A recognition, a pull. I connected with him and booked a session.

I went in braced for more of what I had experienced in the counsellor's office — polite listening, some gentle advice, the careful avoidance of anything that might actually require me to feel something. What happened instead was entirely different. I was introduced to ideas I had never encountered: that we can become trapped in victim mentality without knowing it, that taking radical responsibility for our lives is not the same as blaming ourselves for what was done to us, and — most powerfully, that the past does not simply recede. It repeats. Our unhealed experiences do not stay in the past. They travel forward with us, showing up in our choices and relationships and reactions until we heal them at the source.

Not only was I educated but we did deep transformational work. Right there in the session. I left that room awakened in a way I had not known was possible. The colours felt different driving home. My body felt lighter, as though something I had been carrying for years had been set down without my quite noticing the moment it happened. I had a conscious awareness, for the first time, of the root causes of my patterns — not as concepts, but as felt understanding. Things I knew in my bones.

That session planted the seed that became everything that RCT is today.

— — —

I tell you this story not because I think a healer must have been broken to be of service, but because I think it is important that you understand what I was searching for, and what I kept finding was not quite there. Not in the counsellor's office, where listening without intervention left me more alone than before I walked in. Not in the talk therapy model that would revisit the same experiences week after week without ever quite touching the root of them. Not in the approaches that offered reframes and coping tools and advice without helping the nervous system actually release what it was holding.

There is nothing wrong with any of these approaches in isolation. They have helped many people and they have their rightful place. What I kept noticing — first as a person seeking help, and then as a practitioner beginning to facilitate others — was a gap. A consistent gap between what was happening in sessions and what clients actually needed. Between the surface of the wound and the origin of it. Between managing the symptoms and healing the source.

I started asking questions. Not just to teachers and trainers, but to the clients sitting across from me. What is actually missing here? What would it look like if this truly resolved? What is the moment, the specific, embodied moment, where this all began?

Those questions led me, slowly and then all at once, to Root-Cause Therapy.

What I came to understand, through my own healing and through years of sitting with others in theirs, is that the gap in conventional therapy is not a gap of care or of skill. Most practitioners care deeply. Most are genuinely skilled. The gap is structural. It is built into approaches that work primarily at the level of the conscious mind — with thoughts, with language, with the narratives we tell about our experiences — while leaving the deeper levels of the system largely untouched.

The nervous system does not respond to logic. The body does not release what it is holding because someone explained to it why the holding is no longer necessary. The unconscious mind does not update its beliefs because the conscious mind has been persuaded that they are outdated. For lasting change to happen, we need to work at the level where the wound was originally created — in the body, in the nervous system, in the deep memory that predates language and sometimes even conscious recall.

That is what Root-Cause Therapy does. That is the gap it was built to fill.

And that is why I am so certain — not from theory, but from the lived experience of my own transformation and from watching it happen in thousands of others, that this work is different. Not better in some abstract competitive sense. Different in the specific, essential sense that it goes where other approaches do not reach, and it brings people home to themselves in a way that lasts.

The difference between being heard and being seen is the entire difference between therapy that manages and therapy that transforms.

If you have ever sat with a client and felt that you were circling the real thing without quite landing on it, this book is for you. If you have ever been that client — articulate about your pain, willing to do the work, and yet somehow still stuck. This book is for you. And if you are someone who has simply sensed, without being able to name it yet, that healing ought to feel like more than this, then you are in exactly the right place.

What follows is not a critique of the therapeutic traditions that shaped me and that continue to serve countless people. It is an invitation to go deeper. To ask the questions that the surface cannot answer. To trust that the body knows where the wound is, that the unconscious mind will show us what it is ready to heal, and that the practitioner's most important job is not to provide the answer but to hold the space in which the client finds their own.

We are, all of us, looking for the same thing. A way back to ourselves. Root-Cause Therapy is one of the most precise, compassionate, and powerful maps I have ever found for that journey. The rest of this book is dedicated to teaching you how to read it.

Reflection

> *Have you ever experienced a change that felt real in the moment, but didn't last? What do you think was missing — and what might it mean to heal at the root rather than the surface?*

Your reflection:

Chapter Three: The Neuroscience of Trauma and Healing

I want to offer you a different definition. Not a clinical one, though the science supports everything I am about to say. A human one. One that accounts for the full range of what people actually carry, and why they carry it long after the moment that created it has passed.

Trauma is not defined by the event. It is defined by what the event left behind.

What the Nervous System Remembers

To understand trauma, we need to understand something about how the nervous system works — not in a technical, clinical sense, but in the most practical sense possible. Because once you understand this, you will never again wonder why people cannot simply think or decide their way out of their patterns. You will understand why willpower fails. Why knowing better does not automatically lead to doing better. Why the most intelligent, self-aware people can be completely stuck in behaviours they consciously despise.

When something happens to us that feels threatening, whether that threat is physical, emotional, relational, or existential, the nervous system responds. It does not pause to assess the situation rationally. It responds immediately, because its job is survival. The stress hormones flood the body. The heart rate accelerates. The muscles prepare. Everything non-essential shuts down, and everything that might help us survive is switched on.

This is a beautiful and elegant system when it works as designed. We respond to the threat. We fight, or we flee, or we freeze. The threat passes. And then. This is the crucial part, the nervous system completes the cycle. The activation discharges from the body. The hormones metabolise. The system returns to baseline. We recover.

But sometimes the cycle cannot complete. Sometimes the threat is sustained for so long that there is no recovery window. Sometimes we are too young, or too alone, or too dependent on the very person who is causing the threat to be able to fight or flee. Sometimes what happens is so overwhelming that the system cannot process it in real time, and instead stores it — held in the body, held in the nervous system, held in the deep memory that predates language — waiting for a time when it might finally be safe to be released.

Think of it like a rubber band stretched tight around the soul. We come into this world fairly whole — open, curious, responsive. With each painful experience that we do not have the support or the capacity to fully process, another band is added. Each one a limiting belief, a story about ourselves or the world that formed in the moment of overwhelm: I am not safe. I am not enough. I am not loved. I am to blame. The band does not disappear when the moment passes. It stays, constricting the natural expression of who we are.

Over time, the bands accumulate. Each one sits over the last. The soul — the person we were before things happened to us — is still there, entirely intact, underneath all of it. But the constriction becomes the new normal. We move through life shaped by it: more defended, less free, further from the ease and openness that was our original state. What makes this particularly significant is that the bands do not just restrict — they distort. We feel the past in the present. The nervous system, still carrying the charge of earlier experiences, reads current situations through the beliefs those experiences installed. A familiar tone of voice. A particular kind of silence. A face that resembles someone from long ago. Any of these can activate the stored charge as though the original event is happening now. The client who startles at a gentle question. The person who shuts down in intimacy that should feel safe. The professional who freezes in a meeting room despite years of competence. These are not overreactions. They are the rubber bands doing exactly what they were designed to do — protecting against a threat, but a threat that no longer exists.

This is what I mean when I say that the body time travels. When an emotional charge is activated — whether by a familiar tone of voice, a conflict in an adult friendship, a moment of perceived rejection, or even a feeling that arrives without a clear memory attached — the body does not experience it as something from the past. It experiences it as something happening right now. The nervous system does not distinguish between then and now. It responds to the charge, and the charge is fully alive in the present moment. A thirty-five year old who feels their chest tighten in an argument with a close friend may, beneath the adult surface, be experiencing the emotional reality of an eight year old whose friendships felt unsafe. A person who shuts down when a partner raises their voice may be responding from the nervous system of a two year old who learned that anger meant danger. They have not regressed in the literal sense. They have time-travelled — returned, in their body, to the emotional age at which the original charge was created. And until that original charge is resolved, the time travel will keep happening. The trigger will keep landing in the past rather than the present, because the past is where the unfinished business lives.

And the bands have a second quality that matters enormously for practitioners: they act like a magnet. The unconscious system, in its drive toward completion and healing, keeps drawing toward it the experiences and people that most closely resemble the original wound — not to repeat the suffering, but to create another opportunity to remove the band. This is why patterns repeat. Why the same dynamic appears in different relationships, different workplaces, different decades. It is not bad luck. It is the system trying to finish what it started. In RCT, we go back to the moment each band was placed. We find what the younger self decided in that moment, and we give it what it needed but never received. The belief dissolves. The band releases. And the person becomes a little more free. A little more themselves. RCT gives the system the means to finally do so.

That stored activation is what we call trauma. Not the event. The residue of the event that the system could not complete processing. And it does not diminish simply because time passes. It waits.

> *"Trauma is not what happens to you, but what happens inside you."* — *Dr. Gabor Maté*

The Full Spectrum of Trauma

For a long time, the clinical world drew a sharp line between what researchers sometimes call big T trauma, the acute, undeniable events that produce diagnosable conditions like PTSD, and everything else. The divorce. The humiliation in front of the class. The parent who was physically present but emotionally unreachable. The subtle, chronic experience of never quite feeling good enough, safe enough, loved enough.

These smaller experiences — sometimes called little t traumas — were often treated as insufficiently serious to warrant the same attention. And yet, in my years of practice, I have watched people carry the weight of these so-called smaller traumas with just as much devastation as those who survived acute catastrophic events. In some ways more, because they were never given permission to name what happened to them as real.

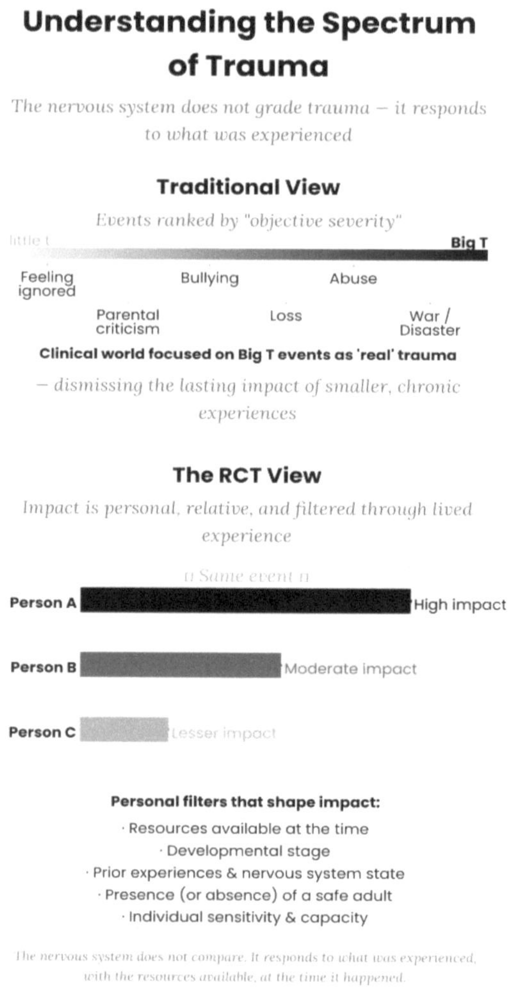

The spectrum of trauma: traditional severity ranking versus the RCT view, where impact is personal, relative, and shaped by individual capacity and context.

Here is what I have come to know. Trauma is not a competition. The nervous system does not grade its responses according to an external scale of how bad things objectively were. It responds according to what it experienced, what resources were available, and what the person was able to process at the time. A child who loses sight of their mother in a shopping centre for twenty minutes may carry the imprint of that event for decades if the emotional charge was never properly completed. Not because the event was catastrophic by any adult standard, but because the child's nervous system experienced it as abandonment — as survival threat, and that experience was never resolved.

Let me walk through what is actually happening in that moment, because it illuminates the entire mechanism of how a childhood experience becomes a lifelong pattern. The child relies on their parent for survival — for food, warmth, safety, the basic conditions of staying alive. This is not metaphor. It is biological fact, encoded in the oldest parts of the nervous system. When that child loses sight of their parent in a crowded shop, the nervous system does not register "a temporary and easily resolvable situation." It registers a survival threat. The primal alarm sounds. Fight, flight, freeze. Chemicals flood the body. The child may cry, or may shut down completely, depending on what their history has taught them is safe to do. But either way, the nervous system is fully activated — and it begins immediately to try to make meaning of what is happening.

The meaning it makes, in that flooded, pre-rational state, becomes a belief: I am alone. I have been abandoned. The world is not safe. And here is the critical point. We know, as adults looking on, that the child was not actually abandoned. The parent was two aisles away. They were reunited within minutes. But the child's nervous system does not care about what we know as adults. It recorded what it experienced: the activation, the fear, the perception of abandonment, the desperate reaching for safety that found nothing there. And it stored all of that as survival data — tagged, encoded, and filed away for future reference.

Children cannot self-soothe. Not in infancy, and not through most of childhood. The capacity for self-regulation develops gradually, with consistent co-regulation from a calm, present adult — and it is not reliably in place until well into the teenage years. When a young child is in a state of high activation and there is no adult available to help them complete the emotional process, the nervous system does what it always does when emotion cannot be safely expressed and completed: it locks it away. The images from the moment get separated from the emotions. The explicit memory becomes hazy. But the stored charge — the body's felt sense of abandonment, of aloneness, of a world that suddenly became unsafe — remains, intact and fully alive, in the nervous system.

Twenty years later, that child is now an adult. They do not remember the shopping centre — or if they do, it feels minor, something they have long since rationalised away. But they find themselves inexplicably anxious when alone. They are drawn into relationships with partners who are emotionally unavailable, not because they want that, but because the nervous system is trying to recreate the original scenario so it can finally resolve it. Small moments of perceived rejection send them into a spiral of panic that seems wildly disproportionate to what actually happened. They cannot explain it. Their therapist, working only at the level of thought, cannot fully reach it either. Because the root is not in the story they can tell about themselves. It is in the stored charge from a moment they can barely remember, waiting for the conditions that will finally allow it to complete.

This is the mechanics of trauma. Not the dramatic, unmistakable kind that everyone can see and name — though that too. The quiet, ordinary kind. The kind that looks, from the outside, like it shouldn't have been a big deal. The kind that the person themselves has often dismissed, because they have been taught, explicitly or implicitly, that their response was out of proportion. It was never out of proportion. It was the precise and faithful response of a nervous system doing exactly what nervous systems do: protecting a young person from a world that felt, in that moment, fundamentally unsafe.

I have seen this play out in session after session. A client who cannot understand why small moments of perceived rejection send them into a disproportionate spiral of panic. A practitioner who knows intellectually that they are safe in their practice but cannot stop bracing for failure. A person who has done years of therapy and can describe their childhood patterns fluently but still cannot seem to change the behaviour those patterns produce. In almost every case, when we go looking for the root, we find not a dramatic catastrophe but a quiet, unremarkable moment, a child left too long without comfort, a teenager shamed in front of their peers, a young adult told in some essential way that they were too much or not enough, that the system never finished processing.

One of the most striking things I have witnessed in this work is this: the people who can explain their patterns most articulately are not necessarily the closest to healing them. I have sat across from psychologists — trained, qualified, intelligent people who know the literature on attachment and trauma better than most — who said exactly this: "I know precisely why I do this. I can trace every pattern to its origin. I've read all the research. And I still cannot stop." This is not a failure of intelligence or self-awareness. It is a fundamental truth about how change actually works. Knowing why does not automatically shift what the body holds. Insight reaches the conscious mind. Healing has to reach the place where the pattern was originally installed — the nervous system, the emotional body, the stored charge of an experience that was never allowed to complete. That is the gap Root-Cause Therapy was designed to close.

This matters enormously for how we approach healing — and for how we approach each other. There is no hierarchy of suffering. We cannot rank pain, compare wounds, or declare one person's experience more worthy of compassion than another's. The scale is entirely personal, entirely relative, and entirely their own.

A client who grew up in material comfort but experienced chronic emotional unavailability may carry wounds just as deep as someone who survived overt violence. The child who was told 'you are too sensitive' every time they cried may have internalised that dismissal in ways that shape every relationship they have as an adult. The person who 'should be over it by now' — because nothing that dramatic happened — is navigating a nervous system that has no interest in external judgements about what was serious enough to leave a mark.

As practitioners — and as human beings — our task is always to meet the person in front of us where they actually are, not where we think they should be given what they've been through. Whatever our own history, whatever our own measure of difficulty, we lay it down completely at the door. We honour the inner experience and reality of the person we are sitting with, no matter what our personal judgement might be of the events themselves.

> *Practitioner Note | The most important thing you can offer a client is the experience of being believed and not ranked. Many people carry years of 'but that's not that bad' — from others, and from themselves. When someone finally enters a space where their nervous system's response is treated as completely valid, regardless of the apparent scale of what caused it, something begins to relax that may never have been able to relax before. That safety is not a luxury. It is the precondition for healing.*

This is why the definition matters. When we expand our understanding of what trauma is and where it lives, we expand our capacity to heal it.

What the Research Confirmed

In the mid-1990s, researchers from the Centers for Disease Control and Prevention partnered with Kaiser Permanente to conduct one of the most significant public health studies ever undertaken. They wanted to understand a simple but profound question: does what happens to us in childhood affect our health as adults? Over seventeen thousand people participated, sharing their childhood experiences and their current health status.

What the researchers found was not subtle. The more categories of adversity a person had experienced in childhood — things like physical or emotional abuse, neglect, living with a parent who struggled with addiction or mental illness, witnessing domestic violence, losing a parent to separation, the greater their risk of almost every significant health challenge in adulthood. Heart disease. Depression. Autoimmune conditions. Substance use disorders. Suicide attempts. The correlation was not slight. It was stark and consistent across the entire dataset.

They called these experiences Adverse Childhood Experiences, and the study became known as the ACE Study[1]. What it told us — what it confirmed in data what healers and trauma workers had been observing for decades — is that childhood adversity does not stay in childhood. It migrates into the body, into the nervous system, into the patterns of thought and behaviour and physical health that shape an adult life. The body keeps the score[17], as the researchers and clinicians who followed this work would come to say.

What I want to draw your attention to, as a practitioner, is not the statistics themselves but what they imply about the people who come to you for help. Most of your clients will have experienced at least one adverse childhood event. Many will have experienced several. And the majority of them will have never connected those early experiences to the symptoms they are presenting with today, the anxiety, the relationship patterns, the physical ailments, the persistent sense that something is wrong even when nothing is visibly wrong.

This is not because they lack intelligence or self-awareness. It is because no one has ever given them the framework to make that connection. And giving people that framework — gently, compassionately, at exactly the right moment in the session — is one of the most powerful things a Root-Cause Therapy practitioner can do.

Nature, Nurture, and the Dance Between Them

There is a question that arises inevitably in any serious conversation about trauma and healing, and I want to address it directly because it matters for how we understand the people we work with and for how we understand ourselves.

Are we the product of what happened to us? Or are we the product of who we were born to be?

The honest answer is: both, always, and in ways that are far more intertwined than either side of the old nature versus nurture debate ever acknowledged. We are not simply running our genes. We are not simply the accumulation of our experiences. We are a continuous, dynamic conversation between the two, and this conversation can be influenced. It can be redirected. That is the scientific basis for everything this book is about.

The field of epigenetics, the study of how environmental factors influence which parts of our DNA are expressed, without changing the underlying genetic code itself — has given us one of the most important insights in the history of human psychology. Genes are not a fixed sentence. They are more like a vast library of possibilities, and our experiences determine which books get taken off the shelf. A person may carry a genetic predisposition toward anxiety. Whether that predisposition becomes debilitating anxiety in their lived experience depends enormously on what happened to them, when, and whether they ever had the resources to heal it.

This cuts both ways. It means that our biology is not our destiny. It also means that our past is not our destiny either because the nervous system, as we now understand it, retains the capacity to change, to learn, and to release what it has been holding. Neuroplasticity, the brain's ability to form new connections and dissolve old ones — is not a metaphor or a motivational concept. It is a physiological reality. And it is the biological foundation upon which every healing in this book rests.

What I tell clients who believe they are simply wired a certain way, that this is just who they are, is this: the statement was never true. It was a conclusion drawn from an incomplete picture. When we heal the wound that the wiring was built around, the wiring changes. Not as a matter of willpower or positive thinking, but as a natural consequence of the nervous system finally being given what it was waiting for.

— — —

How Root-Cause Therapy Understands Trauma

From the Root-Cause Therapy perspective, trauma is not defined by the event itself, but by how the nervous system responds to it and stores it in the body. It is the unresolved activation, the emotional charge that never completed its journey through the system, that creates the ongoing symptoms we see in our clients and in ourselves.

Those symptoms are extraordinarily varied, which is part of why trauma so often goes unrecognised at the root. They include the obvious ones — anxiety, depression, hypervigilance, emotional reactivity — but also the ones that do not immediately announce themselves as trauma responses. Procrastination. Self-sabotage. The persistent inability to receive love without bracing for its loss. Keeping small in life, not going for the goals that matter, maintaining low standards without understanding why. Physical symptoms that defy simple physiological explanation. Compulsions and addictions that no amount of willpower seems able to dislodge.

All of these, in our model, are understood as the nervous system doing its job. They are not pathologies. They are not character deficits. They are adaptive responses to experiences that were never properly processed, and they will continue to drive behaviour until the root is addressed.

This reframe — from symptom as problem to symptom as signal — is one of the most important shifts a practitioner can offer a client. Because when someone understands that their anxiety is not evidence that something is wrong with them, but rather evidence that something unresolved is trying to speak, the entire relationship with the symptom changes. It moves from shame to curiosity. From resistance to willingness. And from willingness, healing becomes possible.

Symptoms are not flaws. They are messengers. Our job is not to silence them — it is to finally hear what they have been trying to say.

In the chapters that follow, we will go deeper into each of these dimensions, the generational patterns that are passed down through family lines and even through DNA, the natal experiences that shape us before we have language, the childhood imprints that determine so much of how we move through adult life. We will explore what the unconscious mind holds, and why accessing it directly; rather than trying to talk around it — is what makes transformation possible at a level that actually lasts.

But before we do any of that, I want you to sit for a moment with the central insight of this chapter. Because it is not just a clinical framework. It is a profound act of compassion.

Every person who comes to you carrying patterns they cannot explain, behaviours they cannot control, feelings that seem disproportionate to the present moment — they are not broken. They are not weak. They are carrying something that was never theirs to carry indefinitely. Something that got lodged in the system at a moment when there was no capacity to process it, and that has been waiting, faithfully and sometimes painfully, ever since.

Your job — our job — is not to fix them. It is to create the conditions in which the body can finally do what it always wanted to do. Complete the cycle. Release what it has been holding. And return the person to the version of themselves that existed before the wound.

That version is always still there. It has never left. It is simply waiting to be found.

Reflection

Your reflection:

Chapter Four: The Emotional Body

This chapter is about that place. About what lives there, how it shapes everything — our choices, our relationships, our capacity for joy and our thresholds for pain, and why accessing it directly, rather than working around it, is what makes the difference between change that lasts and change that doesn't.

What Is Stored There in the nervous system, the organs, the limbic system, the brain.

The unconscious mind is not a dramatic or mysterious thing, despite the language we sometimes use around it. It is simply the part of the mind that operates below the level of our conscious awareness — holding memories, running processes, maintaining beliefs and emotional programmes that were installed, often very early in life, and that continue to influence us whether or not we are aware of them.

Think of it this way. The conscious mind is the part of you that is reading these words right now. It is deliberate, sequential, rational. It can hold a relatively small amount of information at any one time, and it works through language and logic. The unconscious mind is everything else, the vast, largely wordless territory that runs your breathing and your heartbeat, holds every experience you have ever had, and generates the feelings and impulses and automatic responses that arrive in your body before your conscious mind has had a chance to weigh in.

What the unconscious stores is not just memories in the conventional sense. It stores the emotional charge of those memories, the felt sense of what it was like to be in that moment, what we made it mean, and the beliefs we formed about ourselves and the world as a result. A child who is repeatedly criticised does not just remember the specific incidents of criticism. Their unconscious forms a belief from the pattern — I am not enough, or my voice is not welcome, or love is conditional, and that belief begins to operate as a filter through which all subsequent experience is interpreted. By the time that child is an adult, they may have no conscious memory of many of those moments, and yet the belief is everywhere in their life. In the way they shrink in meetings. In the relationships they stay in too long. In the dreams they quietly abandon before anyone can tell them no.

This is not weakness. This is not a failure of self-awareness or intelligence. It is the natural and inevitable consequence of being a human being who was shaped by experiences before they had the capacity to understand or question what those experiences were teaching them.

Why Knowing Is Not Enough

Here is something I have observed consistently across more than a decade of sitting with clients in sessions, and across my own healing journey long before that. People who are stuck are almost never stuck because they lack understanding. Most people who come to therapy, particularly people who have been in therapy for any length of time — are extraordinarily articulate about their patterns. They know that their fear of abandonment connects to their early attachment experiences. They know that their tendency to over-give is rooted in a childhood where love felt conditional on performance. They know. And yet they cannot stop.

This is the gap that conventional approaches so often fail to bridge, and it is the gap that Root-Cause Therapy was specifically designed to close. Because insight — genuine, intelligent, hard-won insight — changes the conscious mind. It does not automatically change the unconscious. And it is the unconscious that is running the show.

The unconscious does not speak the language of logic. It does not update its programmes because someone explained, eloquently and accurately, why those programmes are outdated. It updates when something happens at the level where the programme was originally installed — in the body, in the felt sense, in the emotional memory that predates language and that has been waiting, sometimes for decades, for the experience that was interrupted to finally be completed.

I find it useful to think of stored emotional experiences as bubbles — each one containing an event, the emotion that was activated by it, the meaning that was made in that moment, and the belief that formed as a result. Some of these bubbles are dormant most of the time, sitting quietly in the nervous system, causing no obvious disruption. Others are active — triggered by specific circumstances, relationships, or sensory cues that the nervous system recognises, often without conscious awareness, as resembling the original moment. The person who suddenly feels inexplicably anxious in a particular kind of conversation, the one who finds themselves flooded with sadness at a smell or a song, the practitioner who notices something tighten in their chest when a client expresses a particular kind of emotion — in each case, a bubble has been activated. A stored piece of unfinished experience is making itself known. This is not malfunction. It is the system's persistent, faithful effort to bring to the surface what has not yet been healed — offering it, again and again, until it finally finds the conditions it needs to complete.

This is why so many people describe doing years of talk therapy and feeling, at the end of it, that they understand themselves better but are not fundamentally different. Understanding is not the same as release. Comprehension is not the same as healing. The two can happen simultaneously, and ideally they do — but understanding without somatic release is like being given the map to the exit without ever actually being able to move your feet.

How We Are Wired to Respond

The body leads. Emotion drives thought. Thought produces behaviour.

1 Perception
The body senses for safety or threat before thought occurs

↓

2 Emotion
A chemical signal: feel and / feel but alerted for survival

↓

3 Thought
Rises from emotion into consciousness — not the other way

↓

4 Behaviour
Action driven by emotion + thought combined

Mainstream approaches (CBT) target thoughts directly — but thoughts arise from emotion.

RCT works at the emotional root, which is why the change it produces is lasting.

The sequence the nervous system actually follows: Perception → Emotion → Thought → Behaviour. Conventional approaches (CBT) target thoughts; RCT works at the emotional root.

It is worth pausing on this sequence, because it runs counter to almost everything conventional therapy has taught us. Our bodies are primed to scan our environment constantly — checking whether we are safe, whether the people around us can be trusted, whether this moment resembles something from before. This scanning never stops. It operates below conscious awareness, running all day, every day, even when we would rather it didn't. And you know the feeling: the inexplicable unease around someone you have just met, the sudden tightening in your chest before a conversation you cannot quite justify dreading. That is your body communicating what it has already assessed, before a single conscious thought has formed.

The body registers the perception first. Then it releases an emotion — a chemical signal, a felt sense, a bodily knowing. Only then does thought arrive to name and narrate what the body has already decided. And when the emotion is strong enough, behaviour follows almost automatically, driven not by reasoned decision but by the force of what the body is carrying. Think of a moment when you were genuinely angry with someone. If the emotion was mild, perhaps you noticed a flicker of irritation and moved on. If it was intense, rooted in something old and unresolved, the behaviour that followed — the sharp word, the message you sent and later regretted, the withdrawal that lasted longer than you intended — arrived before you had a chance to choose it. The emotion drove the behaviour. The thought came along to explain it afterwards.

When the body stores a strong emotional experience — particularly one from childhood, when the nervous system had no adult capacity to process it — it does so as survival data. Don't be in this situation again. Don't trust people like that. Don't speak up when it feels like this. That stored data then generates thoughts: I'm not safe. I'm alone. I'm not enough. And those thoughts, combined with the underlying emotional charge, drive the behaviours that puzzled observers — and often the person themselves — call patterns. This is why working at the level of thought alone, however intelligent and rigorous the approach, so rarely produces lasting change. The thought is not the source. The emotion beneath it is. And beneath the emotion is the original perception — the moment when the nervous system concluded something about the world, about safety, about the self, and encoded that conclusion as truth.

When the Pattern Speaks

I want to tell you about a client I worked with — I will call her M because her story illustrates this more vividly than any theoretical explanation could.

M came to me having done years of work on herself. She was intelligent, deeply self-aware, and had read widely on psychology and attachment theory. She could describe her patterns fluently, the way she chose emotionally unavailable partners, the way she became hypervigilant the moment a relationship began to feel secure, the way she would create conflict just as things were getting genuinely good, as though some part of her could not tolerate the peace.

She knew where it came from. She had traced it back, in therapy, to a difficult early relationship with her father — his emotional distance, the way his approval had felt perpetually just out of reach, the way she had learned that love meant longing. She had done the cognitive work. She had the insight. And yet, relationship after relationship, the pattern repeated.

In our first RCT session, we did not begin with the story she knew. We began with the body. I asked her to bring to mind the feeling that arose when a relationship started to feel safe — not the thought about it, not the narrative around it, but the physical sensation. Where was it? What did it feel like? She found it immediately: a tightening in her chest, a kind of bracing, a barely perceptible holding of the breath.

We followed that sensation — not through conversation but through the somatic tracking that is central to RCT, and we asked the unconscious mind to show us when she had first felt this. What surfaced was not the expected memory of her father. It was something earlier and smaller: a moment at around three years old, waking from a nightmare to find her room dark and no one coming. The feeling in her chest was identical. The belief that had formed in that moment, that when things felt frightening, she would be alone — had been living in her nervous system for thirty years, quietly shaping every intimate relationship she had ever entered.

We worked with that memory not by analysing it but by allowing her body to complete what it could not complete at three years old. She allowed herself to feel what the child had felt, to give it space and witness and voice. And then, gently, we brought in what was true, that she was safe now, that the child had survived, that she did not have to keep bracing for an abandonment that had never actually come.

Something shifted. Not dramatically. Not all at once. But the charge in the memory changed. The belief lost its grip. And in the weeks that followed, M noticed something she had not been able to access in years of conscious effort, a capacity to stay present when a relationship started to feel safe, rather than immediately looking for the exit.

That is what working at the level of the unconscious makes possible. Not understanding the pattern from above, but entering it from within, and releasing it at the root.

— — —

How Root-Cause Therapy Accesses the Unconscious

In Root-Cause Therapy, we do not try to override the unconscious mind or argue it into submission. We collaborate with it. We ask it what it is ready to show. We trust that whatever surfaces in a session is exactly what needs to be seen and healed in that moment — not because we are being passive, but because the unconscious has its own intelligence, its own timing, and its own sense of what the system can safely process.

This is one of the things I love most about this work. It is so deeply respectful of the person sitting in front of you. We do not impose. We do not lead the client toward a conclusion we have already decided is correct. We create the conditions — safety, presence, skilled questioning, somatic awareness — in which the unconscious can do what it is always trying to do. Resolve. Complete. Return to wholeness.

— — —

Try It Now: The Awareness Technique

This is a short experiential process used in the RCT course. You can do it right now, wherever you are. Read through the steps first, then put the book down and try it for yourself.

> *Close your eyes.*
>
> *Notice any thoughts you are having — in what direction they are from your head, where they are coming from, and going to. The different trains of thought. Just notice them. Let them go by.*
>
> *Then ask in your mind:*
>
> ***'I wonder where the next thought will come from.'***
>
> *Breathe into it. Wait 5–10 seconds.*
>
> *Now again notice any thoughts you are having. Again, let them go by. Notice what they look like — whether they are pictures or words.*
>
> *And then ask in your mind:*
>
> ***'I wonder what the next thought will look like.'***
>
> ***Or, 'I wonder what my brain will think of next?'***
>
> *Breathe into it again. Wait 5–10 seconds.*
>
> *Now open your eyes.*

What happened?

Most people notice: nothing. A gap. A quiet. And that — that is the point.

Ask yourself: who was the one watching the thoughts? Who was the awareness that noticed when the thoughts slowed or stopped?

That is the conscious mind — not the thoughts themselves, but the pure awareness that observes them. Your thoughts are not you. They are clouds arising from past pain, old experiences, and future anxieties — passing through the sky of your awareness. The sky itself remains unchanged.

This distinction — between the observer and the observed — is at the heart of everything Root-Cause Therapy makes possible. Because when you can witness a thought rather than become it, you create the space in which healing can happen.

— — —

The sway testing that is central to RCT, which we will explore in detail in a later chapter — gives us a direct line of communication with the unconscious. It allows us to ask questions that the conscious mind might not know the answers to, and to receive information about what is actually being held in the body and the deep mind, rather than what the person thinks should be there. It is not a trick or a shortcut. It is a way of listening to the whole person — not just the part of them that speaks in sentences.

And once we have found the root — once the unconscious has shown us the moment where the belief was formed or the emotion was stored, the work of release can begin. Not through analysis, but through allowing. Through creating enough safety in the body that what was frozen can finally begin to move. Through being with what is there, in the way that perhaps no one was able to be with it at the time it was first experienced.

I have witnessed this hundreds of times. The moment a client accesses a memory in the semi-conscious regression, they had not thought about in years, or realises with their whole body — not just their mind, that a belief they have lived by since childhood was never true. The tears that come are not tears of sadness, usually. They are tears of release. Of recognition. Of a burden being set down after a very long time.

What Healing the Unconscious Actually Looks Like

Healing the unconscious is not about excavating the past indefinitely or endlessly revisiting pain. It is about meeting what is there — with compassion, with presence, with skilled support, and giving it what it needed at the time it was formed. Sometimes that is simply witnessing. Sometimes it is the experience of safety that was absent in the original moment. Sometimes it is the wisdom of the adult self being brought back to the child self who made a decision about the world that the adult no longer needs to live by.

What I want practitioners to understand, and what I want anyone reading this for their own healing to feel in their bodies as true, is this: the unconscious mind is not your enemy. It is not a dark or frightening place. It is the part of you that has been faithfully carrying everything you were not yet able to carry consciously, and it has been waiting, patiently and sometimes painfully, for the moment when it would be safe enough to put it down.

Your job as a practitioner is not to force that moment. It is to create the conditions for it. To build enough safety, ask the right questions at the right time, and then step back and trust the extraordinary intelligence of the system you are working with. Because the unconscious knows the way. It has always known the way. It simply needed someone to hold the light while it found its footing.

> *"Until you make the unconscious conscious, it will direct your life and you will call it fate.*[18]*" — Carl Jung*

Jung said this almost a century ago, and it has never been more relevant than it is now, in a world where so many people are living out the same patterns, making the same choices, wondering why nothing seems to change despite everything they know about themselves.

The answer is not more knowledge. It is not more insight. It is not more willpower or better habits or a new therapeutic framework applied at the level of the conscious mind. The answer is to go to where the pattern was created — underneath the words, underneath the story, underneath the years of accumulated meaning, and to meet what is there with enough compassion and skill to finally allow it to move.

That is what the chapters ahead will teach you to do. And that, I promise you, is where everything changes.

Reflection

Your reflection:

— — —

Chapter Five: Consciousness and the Scale of Healing

These were not abstract philosophical questions. They were urgent practical ones, born from the experience of sitting with someone who was suffering and feeling, despite everything I knew, that I was not yet reaching the root. That there was something deeper available, something more complete, and that I had not yet found the map to it.

What followed was years of immersion. Audios, podcasts, books, courses, the best transformative wisdom and therapeutic knowledge I could find. I surrounded myself with it, turned it over, looked for the connections between disciplines that were not often placed in conversation with each other. I watched what happened in sessions, asked clients what had shifted and what had not, and kept refining the approach in response to what I was learning in real time.

Slowly, and then all at once, a philosophy began to emerge. Not a collection of techniques borrowed from elsewhere, but an integrated worldview about what healing is, what it requires, and what becomes possible when all the right conditions are in place simultaneously. That philosophy is what I want to share with you in this chapter because understanding why Root-Cause Therapy works is just as important as understanding how. The how without the why produces a technician. The how and the why together produce a healer.

Principle One: Healing Must Happen on All Levels

The first and most foundational principle of Root-Cause Therapy is one that emerged directly from the failures I observed, both in my own healing and in the approaches I studied. It is simply this: for change to be genuine and lasting, it must happen on all levels of consciousness simultaneously.

What do I mean by that? I mean that a human being is not just a mind, or just a body, or just a spirit. We are all three, always, and they are not separate systems that happen to coexist. They are one integrated system that communicates constantly — upward and downward, inward and outward, and what happens in any one layer affects all the others.

I had experienced energy healing — Reiki and other modalities, that touched something real and created genuine moments of peace and release. But without understanding why the energy had become stuck there in the first place, it tended to return. The root had not been addressed. I had experienced talking therapies that brought extraordinary clarity and insight — I could see the pattern, understand its origins, articulate its effects on my life with precision. But the body still braced. The nervous system still responded as though the threat were present. The understanding had reached the conscious mind but had not penetrated the layers beneath it.

What was needed — what I came to see as the essential missing ingredient in most approaches — was a method that worked with all three levels at once. The conscious mind, with its capacity for awareness, narrative, and meaning-making. The subconscious and unconscious, where the emotional imprints and limiting beliefs are stored. And what I call the superconscious, the soul level, the deeper wisdom, our intuition (or higher mind) the part of a person that existed before the conditioning and that holds the blueprint of who they truly are.

Root-Cause Therapy was built to work at all three levels simultaneously. That is not a small claim. It is the reason the results we see are different from what most single-modality approaches can produce — not because we are more skilled, but because we are working with the whole person rather than one part of them.

Principle Two: The Body Is Not a Passenger

One of the inherited assumptions of Western therapeutic traditions is that the mind leads and the body follows. That if we can change a person's thoughts and beliefs, the body will naturally reorganise itself around those new beliefs. That healing, fundamentally, is a cognitive process.

What I know from my own experience and from thousands of sessions is that this is precisely backwards.

The body is not a passenger in the healing process. It is the terrain. It is where the trauma was stored, where the beliefs live as physical sensations and chronic patterns of tension and holding, where the unconscious communicates everything it is not yet able to express in language. When we ignore the body, when we work only at the level of thought, narrative, and insight — we are doing therapy in a room with most of the lights off. We can see enough to navigate, but we are missing most of what is there.

In Root-Cause Therapy, the body, or the 'soma', hence 'somatic practices' is always in the room. We track sensation. We notice where activation lives, the tightening in the chest, the constriction in the throat, the heaviness in the belly, and we use those somatic signals as a direct line of communication with the unconscious. Not as metaphors. As information. As the body's precise and faithful reporting of what it is still holding and what it needs in order to release it.

This is not a mystical concept. The science of somatic experience, the understanding that the nervous system stores trauma in the body and that the body must be included in the healing process for that trauma to be fully resolved — is now well established. What Root-Cause Therapy offers is a practical, structured way to work with this understanding in every session, from the very first question to the final integration.

Principle Three: The Client's Own Wisdom Is the Destination

This is the principle that I feel most strongly about, and the one that most distinguishes Root-Cause Therapy from approaches that are primarily advice-driven or technique-led. It is also, I think, the one that requires the most from practitioners because it asks us to hold back something that comes very naturally when we care about the person in front of us. It asks us to hold back the answer.

When I first began my own healing journey, I thought I was reaching out for advice. I wanted someone to tell me what to do, to hand me a map, to point toward the exit from my own suffering. And I think most people who enter therapy or coaching have some version of this expectation, that the person with the training and the knowledge will be able to see what they cannot see and tell them what they need to know.

But here is what I have come to understand after more than a decade of sitting in both chairs, as the person seeking help and as the practitioner offering it. Advice, however accurate and well-intentioned, does not integrate the way insight does. When I tell a client what I think is happening for them, I am offering them my map of their territory. And no matter how skilled my cartography, it is not their map. It does not carry the felt authority of their own knowing. It does not land in the body the way their own realisation does. And critically, it does not stay because it was never truly theirs to begin with.

When a client discovers their own wisdom, when they go into the root of the pattern and come back with their own understanding of what happened, what it meant, and what is true now — something entirely different occurs. That insight integrates into the nervous system in a way that borrowed understanding never could. It becomes part of them. It is embodied rather than conceptual. And it changes behaviour not through effort or willpower but because the person has genuinely shifted at the level where the behaviour was being generated.

In Root-Cause Therapy, we are not advisors. We are not experts on the inner landscape of the person sitting across from us. We are guides — skilled, present, deeply trained — but ultimately in service of something that belongs entirely to the client. Their own intelligence. Their own healing. Their own homecoming.

Healing is not about being told what to do. It is about removing the emotional veils that have disconnected us from our own inner knowing. When those veils lift, guidance is not something we seek externally — it rises from within.

Principle Four: The Whole Person, Not the Presenting Symptom

Root-Cause Therapy is a holistic approach — or as I prefer to say, a *wholeistic* one. Because the word holistic has, through overuse, come to carry a certain vagueness. What I mean when I say wholeistic is precise: we look at the whole person, across all dimensions of their life and being, because issues are almost never isolated. They are symptoms of a system. And treating a symptom without understanding the system it belongs to is, at best, temporary relief.

When a client comes to us presenting with anxiety, we do not treat the anxiety. We treat the person. We look at their life across every dimension — their relationships, their work, their physical body, their sense of purpose, their relationship with themselves because any or all of these may be contributing to the anxiety they are experiencing. We look at their history, because the present is always in conversation with the past. We look at their family patterns, because what is unresolved in the generations before us does not simply disappear — it is inherited, in our nervous systems and sometimes in our DNA, until someone in the lineage heals it.

The Testing Sheet, which we will explore in detail in Part Three — is the practical expression of this principle. It is a structured way of looking at the whole person before we go to the root, ensuring that we are not missing any layer that might be contributing to the pattern we are working on. It is one of the things that makes RCT sessions so consistently effective — not because it is complicated, but because it is complete. It does not allow us to miss what is there.

Principle Five: Healing Is a Journey, Not an Event

The final principle I want to introduce in this chapter is one that shapes how we work with clients over time, and how we help them understand their own process. It is the principle that healing is a journey — not a destination, not a transaction, not something that happens in a single session and is then complete.

This does not mean that individual sessions are not profoundly transformative. They are. I have sat with clients who shifted something in sixty minutes that they had been carrying for forty years. Profound change can happen quickly when we are working at the root. But that change exists within a larger process, a process of integration, of new neural pathways forming and old ones releasing their grip, of a person gradually becoming more themselves as the layers of conditioning and trauma are addressed one by one.

I think of it as a general trajectory upward, with the natural rises and valleys of any significant journey. Sometimes after a session a client will feel extraordinary — lighter, clearer, more alive than they have felt in years. Sometimes the days that follow a deep session feel heavy, as the system processes and integrates what was released. Both of these are normal. Both are part of the journey. Our job as practitioners is to help clients understand this, to hold steady when they hit a valley, and to trust, and help them trust, the overall direction of travel.

What I have observed consistently is that when people commit to this journey — not as a quick fix but as a genuine, ongoing commitment to their own healing, the change that happens is not just symptomatic. It is structural. They do not just feel better. They become different. They remember who they really are/were before things happened to them. The patterns that were running them begin to lose their power. The relationships improve, not because the other people changed, but because the person changed. The life begins to reflect, from the outside, the shift that has been happening on the inside.

That is what this work makes possible. Not just relief. Transformation.

— — —

These principles did not come to me all at once. They were not delivered in a single moment of revelation. They were built slowly, through years of practice and refinement, through the questions I kept asking and the answers that kept arriving through the work itself. They are grounded not in theory but in the lived reality of thousands of sessions — in what I have seen work, what I have seen fall short, and what happens when all of these elements are in place simultaneously.

They are also, I want to be clear, not fixed. Root-Cause Therapy is a living methodology. It continues to evolve as our understanding of the nervous system, of consciousness, of trauma and healing deepens. What remains constant is the underlying philosophy, the conviction that every human being carries within them the capacity for complete healing, that the root of every pattern and symptom can be found and addressed, rather than labelled with a lifetime identity, and that when it is, the change that follows is not incremental but foundational.

In the next chapter, we will look at what this philosophy looks like in practice — beginning with one of the most important distinctions in all of this work. The difference between giving a client advice and guiding them to their own wisdom. It is a smaller distinction than it sounds, and a more profound one than almost anything else in this field.

Everything depends on getting it right.

> *Do you connect regularly with your intuition, or your Higher Self? And when you do — or when you don't — what gets in the way of that deeper knowing?*

Your reflection:

PART THREE — THE METHOD

Chapter Six: The RCT Framework

The distinction between advice and guidance is not merely philosophical. It is, in practice, the difference between a session that leaves a client feeling temporarily clearer and a session that changes something fundamental about how they move through their life. It is one of the most important distinctions in this entire body of work, and it is the one I want to explore carefully in this chapter because getting it right will transform the quality of every session you conduct.

What Advice Actually Does

Advice, at its most basic, is when we make a decision or recommendation on behalf of someone else. It is the transfer of our perspective, our experience, our conclusions — offered to another person with the intention of helping them navigate something they are struggling with. And as I said, it can be genuinely useful. There are times when information, context, or a reframe offered at the right moment genuinely serves a client and opens something for them.

But advice has a structural limitation that is almost impossible to overcome, no matter how wise or accurate the advice is. It is not theirs. It was formed in a different nervous system, shaped by a different history, filtered through a different set of experiences and unconscious beliefs. And when a client acts on advice that has come from outside themselves, they are essentially borrowing a map that was drawn for someone else's territory.

This matters enormously in the context of deep healing. Because in the areas where our clients are most stuck, the relationship patterns, the self-worth wounds, the chronic self-sabotage, the problem is almost never a lack of information. Most people who struggle with these things have been given plenty of advice. They have been told to set boundaries, to choose better partners, to value themselves more, to stop people-pleasing. They know what they are supposed to do. And they cannot do it — not because they are weak or resistant, but because the root of the behaviour is operating at a level that advice cannot reach.

There is also a deeper risk in advice-giving that I think practitioners rarely acknowledge. When we offer our perspective as the answer, we are — however unintentionally — reinforcing the client's disconnection from their own inner guidance. We are implicitly saying: you cannot trust your own knowing, so trust mine instead. And for clients who already struggle with self-trust, who have spent years ignoring their own instincts in favour of external validation, this dynamic can actually deepen the wound we are trying to heal.

I have watched this happen. A client who becomes dependent on their practitioner's insights rather than developing their own. A person who gets better at articulating their patterns in the language they have absorbed from sessions but no more able to change them than before. A practitioner who, despite the best of intentions, has gradually become the authority on someone else's inner life, and in doing so, has subtly taken from them the very thing healing is meant to restore.

What Guidance Actually Does

Guidance is something entirely different, and the difference is not just in what we say — it is in the orientation we bring to the entire session. Guidance begins from a premise that advice does not share: that the client already holds the wisdom they need. That the answers we are looking for together are not going to come from us — they are going to come from them, once we have created the conditions in which their own knowing can surface.

This requires a particular kind of presence from the practitioner. A willingness to hold back our own interpretations and conclusions, even when they feel obvious. A trust in the process that is stronger than the impulse to help by providing. A capacity to sit with uncertainty and follow the client's lead rather than directing them toward a destination we have already decided is correct.

It also requires skill because guidance is not passivity. It is not simply listening without responding and calling that non-directive. True guidance involves knowing exactly which question to ask and when to ask it. It involves tracking the client's body as well as their words, noticing where the energy shifts, following the thread that leads toward the root rather than the one that leads toward the story the client is most comfortable telling. It involves knowing when to go deeper and when to stay with what has surfaced, when to introduce a technique and when to simply be present with what is arising.

What guidance produces, when it is done well, is something that advice never can. It produces the client's own realisation — arrived at through their own process, felt in their own body, understood in their own language. And that realisation, because it is theirs, integrates in a way that is qualitatively different from anything we could have offered them from outside. It does not require effort to remember. It does not need to be reinforced in the next session. It becomes part of who they are, because they discovered it themselves, and in discovering it, they also discovered that they were capable of it.

That is the gift of true guidance. Not the answer. The experience of finding their own answer. And with it, the return of something they may not have known they had lost: trust in their own knowing.

Their souls guide us to guide them, their innate intelligence of their own subconscious and body, who does want to heal and bring this person into equilibrium again, is the one that leads the session.

In Root-Cause Therapy, we are co-pilots. The client is always the driver of their own healing. Our job is to know the terrain well enough to help them navigate it — not to take the wheel.

What This Looks Like in Practice

Let me make this concrete, because the distinction can feel abstract until you see it operating in a real session.

Imagine a client who comes to you describing a pattern of overgiving in relationships — always being the one who gives more, who compromises more, who makes themselves smaller to avoid conflict. The advice-based response might sound something like this: it seems like you have learned to prioritise others' needs over your own, probably from early experiences where doing so was necessary for emotional safety. You might want to practise noticing when you are about to override your own needs and pause before doing so.

There is nothing wrong with that response. It may even be accurate. But notice what it does not do: it does not allow the client to discover any of this for themselves. It does not give the body a chance to locate the feeling, or the unconscious mind a chance to show us the moment where the pattern began, or the client's own wisdom a chance to speak about what they actually need in order to change.

The guidance-based approach looks entirely different. It might begin with a question: when you imagine being in that situation — about to give more than you want to give, where do you feel that in your body? And it follows from there: not directing, but tracking. Not interpreting, but asking. Not providing the answer, but creating the conditions for the answer to arise from within.

What often happens, when we follow this thread all the way to the root, is that the client surfaces something neither of us could have predicted. A memory. A belief formed in a specific moment that they had forgotten — or had never consciously held at all. An emotion that has been waiting for decades to be acknowledged. And when they find it themselves, something shifts that no amount of accurate advice could have produced. The body releases what it has been holding. The belief loses its charge. The pattern, which until that moment had felt like an immovable feature of their personality, reveals itself as what it always was: a response to a moment that is now, finally, being completed.

That is guidance. That is what we are practicing in Root-Cause Therapy — not the elegant delivery of insight, but the skilled creation of conditions in which insight can arise from within.

— — —

Real Life Case Study

What follows is shared by one of Jessica's clients, in their own words, after completing a series of Root-Cause Therapy sessions. It is one of the clearest articulations I have encountered of what becomes possible when a practitioner guides rather than advises, when the work reaches not the surface of a person's patterns, but the root of them.

"I felt stuck, spiralling, knowing that I had many beliefs that were too big for me to work through alone. I sought guidance from Jessica, utilising Root-Cause Therapy to explore and shift those beliefs. Root-Cause Therapy is nothing short of life changing. Within four sessions, I had shifted more than 20 deeply ingrained beliefs that had unknowingly shaped my reality, holding me back in ways I never realised. Many of those beliefs were deeply rooted and had dictated my actions, relationships, and self-worth for most of my life. That was until I chose to challenge them.

I had constantly repeated patterns without knowing why or even where they originated from. I felt a heaviness, imprisoned in an outdated version of myself, ruled by beliefs that were embedded from ancestral lineage. We explored the beliefs, and as they dissipated, there was a feeling of lightness and freedom. It wasn't just a case of identifying the belief — but healing them at the core. The feeling of letting go of the beliefs that had weighed me down was empowering. Curating a version of myself without limiting beliefs, leaning into possibilities that I never imagined before. Unveiling the truest version of myself.

Jessica holds space for you to feel safe and supported. She guides you beautifully throughout the process, allowing you the time and space to explore the event at the core of the belief, reminding you that you are safe if the event becomes intense, encouraging you to lean into and feel the emotions in order to release them. Everlasting change is possible."

— Client of Jessica K., RCT Certified Practitioner

Read that again slowly. Twenty deeply ingrained beliefs — beliefs that had been dictating this person's actions, relationships, and sense of self-worth for most of their life — shifted in four sessions. Not because Jessica told her client what to believe instead. But because she created the conditions in which her client could find their way to the truth themselves. She held space. She guided. She reminded her client that they were safe to feel. And her client did the rest.

That is the power of guidance over advice. That is what becomes possible when a practitioner has the skill and the trust to step back from the impulse to provide, and instead to create the conditions in which the client's own wisdom can finally be heard.

If you are interested in working with Jessica Kyriacou, you can find her at @byjessicak_ on Instagram

— — —

The Danger of the Clever Reframe

There is one more dimension of this distinction I want to address, because I see it operating in the work of many well-intentioned practitioners, including in my own early practice, before I understood what was missing.

Reframing is a technique borrowed primarily from cognitive approaches to therapy, and it involves helping a client see their experience, belief, or situation through a different lens. It can be genuinely powerful when used at the right moment. But reframing without releasing is, I have come to understand, a form of advice in disguise. It says: here is a different way to think about what happened to you. And the implicit message underneath it is: your current way of thinking about it is the problem, and this new perspective is the solution. Reframing can cause more disconnection from the body, more dissociation, which is the opposite of healing, or to become 'whole'.

The issue is not with the perspective being offered. It may be entirely accurate. The issue is that reframing operates at the level of the conscious mind — it changes the story, but it does not move what is held in the body. And when the body is still holding the original emotional charge of the experience, no amount of reframing will dislodge it. The client leaves with a better story about the same wound. The wound itself remains.

I know this from my own body. Early in my training, before I understood what I was doing, I tried to reframe my way out of the things I was carrying. I was taught it was the tool, the intervention, the route to a new perspective and a better life. For a short time, it seemed to work — I could tell a different story, hold a different frame. But the feelings did not move. They went quiet. I had pushed them further down into the unconscious, disconnected a little more from my body, widened the gap between what I told myself I felt and what I actually felt. This is not a sidestep to healing. It is a form of fragmentation — and fragmentation, over time, is its own wound. Reframing without releasing is like cutting the top off a weed and calling it gardening. The roots remain. And from those roots, the same plant grows back, often denser and more entangled than before. In Root-Cause Therapy, we pull the weed out properly — we find the root, we release the stored charge, and then we allow the genuine reframe to arise from within the person themselves, because a reframe that comes from inside the healing is not a new thought. It is a new truth.

In Root-Cause Therapy, we do not lead with the reframe. We lead with the release. We allow the emotions that have been stored to move through the body, to be witnessed and completed, before we ask what understanding or wisdom naturally arises from that release. And what we have found, consistently and without exception, is that when the emotional charge clears, the client does not need us to offer them a new perspective. They find their own, and it is always more precise, more personal, and more deeply integrated than anything we could have given them.

The reframe that comes from within is not just a new thought. It is a new truth, felt in the body, arrived at through direct experience. That is the difference. And that difference is everything.

Learning to Trust the Space

For many practitioners, especially those who came into this work from advice-based traditions, the shift to guidance can feel uncomfortable at first. It can feel like doing less, like withholding something that could help, like sitting with uncertainty when you could be offering something solid.

What I want to offer you — not as advice, but as the truth of my own experience — is that this discomfort is worth moving through. Because on the other side of it is something extraordinary: the experience of watching a client find their own way home, in the presence of your skill and your holding, without needing to borrow your map to get there.

When you guide rather than advise, you give your clients something that outlasts the session. You give them the experience of trusting themselves. Of discovering that their own knowing is not only accessible but reliable. Of understanding that the wisdom they have been seeking externally was always present within them, waiting only for the conditions in which it was finally safe to be heard.

That experience — once a client has had it — becomes its own resource. It changes not just how they feel after a session, but how they move through their life. They become more capable, not more dependent. More autonomous, not more reliant on you for the next piece of insight. More whole.

That is what we are building toward, in every session and across the entire arc of the therapeutic relationship. Not a client who needs us indefinitely. A client who has been guided back to themselves so completely, so thoroughly, that they no longer need to be guided at all.

That is the highest expression of this work. And it begins, every time, with the choice to guide rather than to advise.

Reflection

Your reflection:

— — —

Chapter Seven: The Testing Sheet

In many circles, particularly in the more conventional corners of the therapeutic world — holistic has become synonymous with alternative, which has become synonymous with unproven, which has become synonymous with not quite serious. And I understand how that happened. The word has been stretched to cover everything from genuinely evidence-based integrative approaches to crystals and unverifiable claims, and somewhere in that stretching, the original meaning got lost.

So let me give it back its meaning. Because what I am describing when I use the word holistic is not a philosophy that competes with science. It is one that insists on taking science seriously enough to include everything the body of evidence actually supports, which is considerably more than mainstream approaches tend to acknowledge.

Holistic, as I use it, means whole. Not whole as in a bit of everything thrown together, but whole in the precise sense: looking at a person as the genuinely complex, multidimensional, deeply interconnected system that they are, and refusing to treat any single part of that system as though it existed in isolation from the rest.

That is what this chapter is about. And it is the lens through which everything that follows in this book should be read.

What It Means to See the Whole Person

Most therapeutic and coaching approaches, however skilled, tend to work primarily with one dimension of a person at a time. Talk therapy works primarily with the narrative mind, the stories we tell about our experiences, the meanings we have made, the insights we can arrive at through language and reflection. Coaching works primarily with the future-focused conscious mind, where we want to go, what is in the way, how to build the motivation and strategy to get there. Even somatic approaches, which have done so much to bring the body back into the conversation, sometimes work with the physical dimension without fully integrating the spiritual or the relational.

Where RCT Works

The three levels of the human system

Nervous System & Body
Somatic sensation · Stress hormones · Physical symptoms

·And here
Somatic releasing, nervous system co-regulation, body-held trauma

Unconscious Mind
Stored memories · Emotional patterns · Core beliefs

·RCT reaches here
Deep healing, belief resolution, timeline healing, inner child work

Conscious Mind
Thoughts & awareness

·Most therapies reach here
Talk therapy, CBT, coaching, counselling

RCT addresses all three levels simultaneously — which is why the change it produces is structural, not temporary.

Where RCT works — across all three levels of the human system simultaneously.

Root-Cause Therapy was built on the premise that this separation is not just incomplete — it is, in a meaningful sense, impossible. A human being cannot be divided into their mind on one side and their body on the other, their past in one room and their future in another, their conscious awareness in the foreground and their unconscious in a locked basement. These things are one continuous system, communicating constantly, each part affecting all the others in ways that are real and measurable and consequential.

When a client comes to us carrying what presents as a career problem, a pattern of self-sabotage that keeps derailing their professional life — we do not treat the career. We look at the whole person. We ask about their relationships, because how we attach to people tends to mirror how we attach to our ambitions and opportunities. We ask about their body, because the nervous system that is bracing against vulnerability in intimacy is the same nervous system that is bracing against visibility in professional life. We ask about their history, because the child who learned that standing out was dangerous does not leave that lesson at the door when they walk into an adult workplace.

We look at everything, not because we are going to work on everything simultaneously, but because understanding the whole system is what allows us to find the root. And the root, once found, tends to resolve the pattern across all dimensions at once. That is the efficiency, and the elegance — of working holistically.

Wholeistic: Spirit and Science Together

I prefer the word *wholeistic*, and I spell it that way deliberately. Because I want to keep the wholeness visible in the word itself, to resist the slide toward vagueness that holistic has undergone, and to signal something specific: that what we are working with includes not just the mind and the body but the spirit. The soul level. The dimension of a person that exists beneath and beyond the conditioning, the survival adaptations, the accumulated layers of who they learned to be, and that holds, quietly and persistently, the blueprint of who they actually are.

This may sound, to some readers, like a departure from science. It is not. What I mean by spirit is not a religious concept, though it can be held within a religious or spiritual framework if that is meaningful to the client. What I mean is the deepest layer of self, the one that the unconscious mind, when we work with it directly, tends to call the higher self or the true self. The part of a person that knows, even when the rest of them has forgotten. That holds the wisdom that the trauma obscured. That has been present all along, waiting for the layers on top of it to be addressed so that it can finally be heard.

When I work with clients, I am always working toward this layer. Not because it is the starting point — it rarely is — but because it is the destination. The moment in a session when a client accesses something that feels, to them, like coming home. Like recognising themselves after years of being a stranger to themselves. That is the superconscious speaking. And when it does, the change it produces does not need to be reinforced or maintained. It is simply true. It integrates naturally, because it is not a new idea being installed from outside — it is an original truth being remembered from within.

This is what I mean by spirit and science together. The science gives us the mechanism, the neurobiology of trauma, the physiology of somatic release, the evidence base for working with the unconscious. The spirit gives us the destination, the return to wholeness, to authenticity, to the self that was there before the world began its work of shaping us into something more manageable.

Neither alone is sufficient. Together, they are transformative.

What Eastern and Western Traditions Each Got Right

We are living in a remarkable moment in the history of healing. For the first time in human history, the knowledge traditions of East and West, which developed largely in isolation from each other across centuries — are genuinely in conversation. The boundaries between them are dissolving, not through either side abandoning its rigour, but through a growing recognition that the questions they are each answering are not different questions. They are the same question, approached from different angles, with different tools, and arriving at complementary rather than contradictory insights.

Western medicine and psychology gave us the scientific method, the randomised controlled trial, the neuroscience of trauma and attachment, the pharmacology that can stabilise a person in crisis while longer-term healing work begins.

These are not small gifts. They have reduced suffering at scale in ways that no previous era of human history could match.

Eastern traditions gave us something different but equally essential: centuries of accumulated practical wisdom about the relationship between mind and body, between individual experience and collective pattern, between the physical symptoms of a person and the emotional and spiritual dimensions that are always present beneath them. Acupuncture. Ayurveda. Meditation practices that predate neuroscience by millennia but that modern neuroscience is now demonstrating have measurable, significant effects on brain structure and nervous system regulation.

At The Centre for Healing, we do not choose between these traditions. We draw from both, with discernment and without dogma, because a person in front of us is too complex and too precious to be served by only half of what is available. We hold the scientific rigour and the ancient wisdom simultaneously. We take the evidence base seriously and we also take seriously the things that the evidence base has not yet found a way to measure, the moments in sessions that cannot be quantified but that practitioners and clients both recognise, beyond any doubt, as real.

Root-Cause Therapy sits precisely at this intersection. It is informed by the neuroscience of trauma and the clinical research into somatic approaches. It is also informed by the understanding, held across many ancient traditions, that healing is ultimately a return to wholeness, and that the obstacle to that return is always some form of disconnection from the self that we were before we were wounded.

Where Therapy Ends and Coaching Begins, and Why RCT Lives in Between

One of the questions I am asked most frequently by practitioners considering the RCT certification is about the distinction between what we do and what conventional therapy or coaching does. It is a fair and important question, and I want to answer it carefully — not to position RCT competitively, but because understanding the distinction clarifies something essential about what makes this approach uniquely suited to the depth of work we are attempting.

Therapy, in its conventional forms, works primarily with the past. It helps people understand their history, process their experiences, develop insight into their patterns, and build resources for navigating their emotional lives. At its best it is profound. At its most common, it tends to be open-ended, oriented toward understanding rather than resolution, and focused on managing symptoms rather than healing their origin.

Coaching, in its conventional forms, works primarily with the future. It is goal-oriented, action-focused, and concerned with closing the gap between where a client is and where they want to be. It tends to be relatively brief, structured, and outcome-driven. At its best it produces remarkable momentum. At its most common, it works at the surface of a person's conscious ambitions without addressing the unconscious resistance that so often undermines them.

Root-Cause Therapy is neither of these things, and both. It takes the future orientation of coaching, the clear intention, the goal, the vision of how the client wants to feel in their life, and uses it as a map for the session. And then it takes the depth orientation of therapy, the willingness to go into the past, to work with what is held in the body, to address the root rather than the symptom, and applies it with precision to whatever is in the way of the goal.

The result is an approach that is simultaneously more focused than conventional therapy and more transformative than conventional coaching. Clients do not just feel clearer. They shift. And they shift in ways that last, because we are not working with the branches. We are working with the root.

In Root-Cause Therapy, we don't treat the label. We treat the person — symptom by symptom, root cause by root cause — until what was holding them back has been released, and what was always true about them can finally emerge.

In Defence of the Word "Alternative"

I want to say something directly to any reader — practitioner or client, who has been taught to be suspicious of approaches that sit outside the mainstream. Because I think that suspicion, however understandable, is costing people access to help that works.

Alternative simply means different from what is currently dominant. It does not mean unproven. It does not mean ineffective. It does not mean that the practitioner using it has abandoned their commitment to the wellbeing of the people they serve. Some of the most powerful healing approaches available today are described as alternative simply because they have not yet been processed through the particular machinery of randomised controlled trials — not because the evidence of their effectiveness is absent, but because that evidence exists in forms that the machinery was not designed to measure.

I have personally sought medical help for issues that conventional medicine could not resolve, and found resolution through approaches that would be described as alternative. I have sat with clients who had undergone test after test in conventional medical settings with no answers, who found relief and healing through modalities that a standard referral pathway would never have offered them. I have watched symptoms that had been managed with medication for years dissolve when their emotional root was addressed — not because the medication was wrong, but because medication was never able to reach what was generating the symptom.

I am not asking you to abandon discernment. I am asking you to apply it evenly — to be as willing to question the limitations of conventional approaches as you are to question the claims of alternative ones. Because the people who come to us for help deserve practitioners who are not ideologically limited in what they are able to offer. They deserve practitioners who can draw from the full range of what is known, proven, ancient, and emerging, and who have the training and the wisdom to know which part of that range is most needed, for this person, in this moment.

That is what a wholeistic approach makes possible. And that is what Root-Cause Therapy is built to deliver.

— — —

Practitioner Spotlight

Jenna Smith

RCT Certified Practitioner — Wisconsin, United States

Jenna's story is one of the most powerful illustrations I know of what a truly wholeistic approach to healing makes possible — not just for the clients we serve, but for the practitioners themselves. She shares it here in her own words.

> *"Root-Cause Therapy didn't just change how I worked within my practice. It changed how I live.*

Long before I had the language for it, I was always searching for the root of things. Even as a child, I questioned what lived beneath behaviour. As I grew older — becoming a mother, moving through my own spiritual awakening, leaving the medical field to build my own practice — I began to see clearly that behaviours are not the problem. Vices are not the thing to replace with another bandage. They are protective responses to something deeper. I intuitively understood this. But I didn't yet have a structured, somatic way to access and release what lived underneath.

In my own life, years of disordered eating, alcoholism, and shame-based 'not enough' parts became woven into that story. They helped me cope and survive during seasons when my nervous system didn't feel safe enough to hold the emotions moving through me. For decades, I tried to manage the behaviour. What Root-Cause Therapy gave me was the ability to gently and directly access the pain beneath it, driving it.

Through this work, I learned how to feel without being overwhelmed. I learned how to release stored emotional charge rather than carry it. I learned that when you truly heal at the root, the cycles connected to coping mechanisms begin to dissolve naturally. My perspective shifted. Sobriety was no longer the goal. Wholeness was. Integration was. And sobriety became a byproduct of healing.

As a practitioner now, Root-Cause Therapy allows me to hold clients in a way that deeply honours the body's intelligence and bio-individuality. There is no fixing. No pathologising. Only compassionate uncovering, witnessing, and releasing what was never meant to be carried alone. This work restores the self-love, self-trust, and self-connection that have long been central in my practice. It brings people back into relationship with their own nervous system. And it reminds us that symptoms are not flaws — they are messengers.

Root-Cause Therapy gave me the tools to come home to myself. Now it is an honour to guide others home as well."

— Jenna Smith, RCT Certified Practitioner, https://naturallyempoweredliving.com/

Sobriety as a byproduct of wholeness rather than a goal in itself. That one sentence contains the entire philosophy of this chapter. When we work with the whole person, when we address not the behaviour but the wound the behaviour was protecting, the behaviour changes naturally, because it no longer needs to serve the function it was serving. That is what wholeistic healing looks like in a human life. That is what becomes possible when we stop treating the symptom and start treating the root.

— — —

From Philosophy to Practice

Everything in this chapter, the insistence on wholeness, the integration of spirit and science, the refusal to separate the body from the mind or the past from the present — finds its practical expression in the method that the second half of this book is dedicated to exploring.

The Testing Sheet, which we will meet in detail in Part Three, is the *wholeistic* philosophy made tangible. It is the structured way we look at the whole person before we go to the root — mapping every dimension of their life, every layer of their experience, every place where something might be contributing to the pattern we are working on. It is not a bureaucratic checklist. It is an act of genuine care, the practitioner's commitment to not missing anything, to seeing the person in front of them as fully and accurately as possible before the deeper work begins.

The healing protocols that follow from it carry the same philosophy: the understanding that the emotional, the physical, the relational, the generational, and the spiritual are not separate territories to be visited in sequence but dimensions of a single, integrated human life. And that when we work with that life as the whole, irreducibly complex, inherently worthy system that it is, the healing that becomes possible is of a different order entirely from what any partial approach can reach.

That is where we are headed. And everything we have covered so far, the story of how this work came to be, the science of what trauma is and where it lives, the philosophy of guidance over advice and wholeness over symptom management — has been preparing you for it.

The method is waiting. Let us begin.

Reflection

Your reflection:

Chapter Eight: Healing, Accessing the Database of Memories

This is not a metaphor. It is not a therapeutic exercise designed to make you think about time in a new way. It is a direct communication from your unconscious mind about how it actually stores and organises your experience. And it is the foundation of one of the most powerful tools in Root-Cause Therapy.

We call it the Timeline.

What the Timeline Is

The concept of the Timeline was originally developed within the field of Neuro-Linguistic Programming in the 1980s[9], building on earlier work in hypnotherapy and the understanding that the unconscious mind stores memories with a spatial, directional quality. When I trained in Neuro-Linguistic Programming (NLP) and Timeline Therapy[14], I encountered this idea early, and it immediately rang true, both from my own experience and from what I was observing in the clients I was beginning to work with.

In Root-Cause Therapy, the Timeline is the structure through which the unconscious mind organises all of its experiences —

past, present, and future, as a continuous line in space. When we work with the Timeline in a session, we are not asking the client to imagine something that doesn't exist. We are asking them to access something that already does, a real organisational structure that the unconscious mind uses to file, retrieve, and process every experience it has ever had.

Elicitation of the Timeline

Every person organises time differently – discover your client's unique direction.

Ask: "Imagine a memory from this morning – where does it feel like it is, in relation to your body?"

Elicitation of the Timeline — every person organises time differently; discovering your client's unique direction is the first step.

This matters enormously, because it means that by working with the Timeline, we can do something that no amount of conscious reflection or conversation can achieve: we can go directly to the stored memory of a past experience — not the story about it, not the current interpretation of it, but the actual event as the unconscious holds it, and we can work with it there. At the source. At the root.

That is why Timeline work is central to RCT rather than peripheral to it. It is not a technique we reach for occasionally. It is the mechanism through which every past healing session operates.

How the Unconscious Mind Stores Time

To understand why the Timeline is so powerful, it helps to understand something about how the unconscious mind stores experience differently from the conscious mind.

The conscious mind stores memories sequentially and interpretively. It holds a narrative, a story about what happened, shaped by subsequent experience, coloured by the meanings we have made, edited by the parts of ourselves that found certain truths too difficult to hold. It is, in other words, a reconstruction. And reconstructions, however accurate they feel, are always filtered through the present self.

The unconscious mind stores differently. It stores the emotional charge of an experience, the raw felt sense of what it was like to be in that moment — largely intact, regardless of how much time has passed or how much the conscious narrative has shifted around it. This is why someone can describe a childhood experience with complete composure at the conscious level — they have processed the story, and yet the moment we access the unconscious memory, the emotion is as present and as alive as it was the day it was created. It has been waiting, preserved in the body, unchanged.

This is the mechanism that makes the Timeline so clinically powerful — and it is also the mechanism that explains something clients often struggle to understand about their own reactions. When a trigger activates a stored charge, the body does not experience that charge as a memory. It experiences it as present reality. The nervous system has no internal clock that marks certain feelings as belonging to the past. An emotional charge stored from age two is accessed with the same immediacy and urgency as if the event were happening now. This is why a grown adult can find themselves in the emotional reality of a toddler — not metaphorically, but somatically. The body has time-travelled. It has returned to the moment the charge was created, and it is responding from the emotional maturity, the resources, and the perspective available at that age. Understanding this is not just theoretically interesting. It changes everything about how we approach our clients. The goal of Timeline work is not to re-visit the past intellectually. It is to go back to the precise moment the body is already returning to every time it is triggered — and finally, in that moment, to give the younger self what it needed and never received. When we do that, the time travel stops. Because the unfinished business is finished.

The Timeline gives us a pathway to that stored material. When a client floats up above their Timeline in a session, when they access that elevated perspective from which the whole line of their experience becomes visible — they are not imagining.

They are using a real perceptual capacity that the unconscious mind already possesses, and accessing it in a structured, guided way that allows the healing work to proceed with extraordinary precision.

The First Session: Mapping the Timeline

In every client's first session involving Timeline work, we begin by mapping their personal Timeline before we do anything else. We ask the unconscious mind — not the conscious, not the thinking self — to show us where the past is and where the future is. We ask the client to point, without overthinking it, in the direction that simply feels right.

What we are doing here is several things simultaneously. We are establishing the client's individual Timeline structure, which varies from person to person. We are beginning to build a direct working relationship with the unconscious mind — communicating with it on its own terms, in spatial and somatic language rather than verbal language, and establishing that it is safe to do so. And we are orienting the client to an experience of their own inner landscape that many of them have never had before, the recognition that their history exists not only as narrative but as a living, spatially organised structure within them.

We then ask the unconscious mind to float up above the Timeline — above the present moment, and to explore both directions. We go out toward the past, noticing what is there, what colours or qualities the client perceives. We go out toward the future. We get a sense of the whole line. And then we bring the client back to the present, oriented, familiarised with the terrain, ready for the deeper work of the session.

> ***Practitioner Note |*** *In first sessions, note the exact directions the client indicates for past and future — many practitioners mark this with a small diagram on the Testing Sheet. This becomes the consistent map for all subsequent sessions with that client. The Timeline structure tends to remain stable once established.*

Going to the Root: How the Healing Actually Works

Once the client is oriented above their Timeline, the real work begins. We have identified — through the Testing Sheet process we will explore in the next chapter, a specific emotion, limiting belief, or trauma imprint that is ready to be addressed. We ask the unconscious mind a question that is, in its simplicity, one of the most powerful questions in all of this work:

What is the root cause of this problem, the first event, which, when healed, will cause the problem to disappear?

And then we ask: was it before, during, or after your birth?

I want to pause here, because this question stops many practitioners and clients in their tracks the first time they encounter it. Before birth? What does that mean? Are we talking about past lives? Generational trauma? Natal experience?

The answer is: all of the above, and the unconscious mind knows which it is. We do not decide in advance. We do not impose a framework. We simply ask, and we trust what arises because what arises is always precisely what is ready to be healed in this moment. Sometimes the root is in this lifetime, perhaps at two years old, perhaps at sixteen. Sometimes it is in a natal experience — something that happened in the womb, or during the birth itself, that created an imprint before the client had any conscious capacity to interpret or process it. Sometimes it is genealogical, a pattern that has been carried through the family line, sometimes for many generations. And sometimes it presents as a past life experience. Whatever framework a client holds for that — spiritual, metaphorical, or simply unknown, the unconscious works with it as real, and the healing that follows is real regardless of the philosophical questions it raises.

Once we have established when the root event is, we ask the unconscious mind to float up above the Timeline, travel to that point in time, and drop down into the event itself — so the client is experiencing it from the inside, looking through their own eyes, feeling what was felt. Not as a spectator at a safe remove, but as a participant. Present with what is actually there.

> ***Practitioner Note |*** *The instruction to look "through your own eyes" is deliberate and important. It places the client*

> *fully inside the experience rather than observing it from a distance, which allows the emotional charge to be fully accessed and therefore fully released. If a client is dissociating or the material feels too intense, you can temporarily move them to an observer position — but the release happens most completely from the associated, inside-the-experience position.*

The Release: What Actually Happens in the Event

Once the client is in the event, we work with what is there. We identify the emotions or sensations that are present, where they live in the body, and how intense they feel on a scale of zero to ten. And then, and this is the part that surprises most people the first time they witness it — we turn them up.

We ask the client to go right into the emotion, to amplify it like a volume dial being turned upward. We guide them gently but firmly somatically into the feeling rather than away from it, all the way up to its peak intensity, and then we hold the space as the emotion begins, naturally and inevitably, to move and release.

This is counterintuitive. Everything in our cultural conditioning tells us that the way to handle intense emotion is to soothe it, manage it, distract from it, reduce it. What we are doing is the opposite, and the reason it works is precisely because it is the opposite of what the emotion has been receiving for years or decades. The emotion was interrupted at the moment it was created. It could not complete its natural arc. It has been held in the system in a state of incompletion ever since. When we allow it to intensify fully, when we give it the space and the witness it never had — it completes. It moves through. It dissipates.

Clients consistently report something that sounds paradoxical until you experience it: that going fully into the feeling is the fastest way out of it. Not because we forced it out, but because we finally let it finish in the safety of the clients own time and rhythm They are still conscious and awake, so they are still in control. There is safety built into the process.

Going fully into the feeling is the fastest way through it. Not because we push it out — but because we finally let it complete.

The Learnings: What the Event Has to Teach

Once the emotional charge has cleared, and we always ensure it has cleared completely before moving on, not just reduced — something interesting happens. The client's perception of the event changes. Without the emotional charge distorting their view, they can see what actually happened more clearly. And they can access something that was not available to them while the emotion was present: the learnings.

We ask the unconscious mind and the higher self, that deeper layer of wisdom that holds a broader perspective on the experience — what can be learned from this event. What is important to know? What does this younger self, or this ancestor, or this past life self, need to understand in order for the healing to be complete?

What emerges in this part of a session is often extraordinary. Clients who went into an event carrying shame come out with understanding. Clients who went in carrying rage come out with compassion — for themselves, and sometimes for the people who caused the wound. The learnings are never delivered by the practitioner. Only sometimes suggested if needed. They arise from within the client themselves, which is precisely why they integrate so completely. They are not a reframe we have offered. They are the client's own wisdom, finally audible now that the noise of the unprocessed emotion has cleared.

> ***Practitioner Note |*** *Keep gently asking "anything else?" during the learnings phase. Clients will often think they are done and then — with one more prompt — access something that turns out to be the most important piece. Don't rush this part. The learnings are where the cognitive and conscious integration happens alongside the somatic release, and both are necessary for change that lasts.*

Preserving the Learnings and Returning to Now

Once the learnings are complete, we ask the unconscious mind to do something specific and essential: to preserve the learnings, and then to begin floating back toward the present along the Timeline — but only as quickly as it releases the emotion and the limiting belief on every connected event all the way back to Now.

This instruction matters deeply, and I want you to understand why. A root cause event is rarely a single isolated moment. It is the first in a chain, a series of experiences that compounded the original imprint, each one adding another layer to the belief or the emotional pattern. When we heal the root and then travel back to the present along the Timeline, we are allowing all of those connected events to be swept clean simultaneously. Not one by one, in separate sessions, but in a single movement of release, as the unconscious follows the chain from root to present and restores what was distorted at each point along the way.

This is one of the reasons RCT produces results so quickly relative to approaches that address experiences sequentially. We are not working on individual memories one at a time. We are healing the root and allowing the entire chain to resolve.

When the client is back above the present moment, we check the original emotion or belief. What was a ten may now be a zero. What was a deeply held conviction — I am not safe, I am not enough, I cannot be loved — may now feel simply untrue. Not intellectually refuted, but viscerally, somatically, obviously no longer real. The client's nervous system has updated. The pattern has lost its root, and without its root, it cannot sustain itself.

How Trauma Shapes Behaviour

A perception in the body creates an emotional response — which drives thought and behaviour

Perception
The way the experience is received by the nervous system

↓

Emotion
A feeling stored in the body

↓

Thoughts
Stories the mind builds around the feeling in the body

↓

Behaviour
Automatic patterns that arise from and reinforce the feeling

Without addressing the original perception, changes in thoughts and behaviour remain surface-level — and temporary.

How trauma shapes behaviour: a perception in the body creates an emotional response, which generates thought and drives behaviour. RCT works at the level of perception — where lasting change becomes possible.

The Future Timeline: Healing Forward

The Timeline does not only reach into the past. It extends into the future as well, and working with the future dimension of the Timeline is one of the most distinctive and transformative aspects of RCT.

Future healing sessions work differently from past healing sessions. Rather than going to a specific memory to release a stored charge, we ask the unconscious mind and higher self to take the client to a point in their future, the most optimal and helpful moment for them to see today, and to allow them to experience it fully. To feel what it feels like to be there. To receive the wisdom and advice that their future self, having already navigated what the present self is currently struggling with, has to offer.

What clients access in future healing sessions is consistently moving. They see versions of themselves that are whole, free, purposeful — versions that may have seemed impossible from the perspective of the wounded present self. And in seeing them, and feeling what it feels like to be them, something in the nervous system begins to reorganise toward that possibility. Not as a visualisation technique or an affirmation, but as a genuine experience of a future that the unconscious now knows is real.

Future sessions are typically offered later in the healing journey, once a significant amount of past material has been addressed and the system has more capacity for expansion. They are also invaluable for clients who are struggling with purpose, direction, or a sense that the future feels blank or frightening. The Timeline stretches in both directions, and both directions hold resources for healing.

The whole point of helping the client heal the past and future, is so they can be present in the now. The body is constantly pulled on the strings of the past and future via trauma, past pain and future anxiety and worries. Releasing these allows them to come back to peace and presence, but with more wisdom that when they started.

> ***Practitioner Note |** If the unconscious mind indicates it is not ready to visit the past in a given session, always check whether it wants to go into the future instead. Some sessions naturally call for future work, and the unconscious knows which direction is most needed. Trust that guidance and follow it.*

What Clients Experience

I want to speak to what this actually feels like from the inside, because no technical description fully captures it, and because understanding the client's subjective experience is what allows practitioners to hold the space for it well.

For many clients, the first time they float above their Timeline is one of the most unusual experiences they have ever had. Some see it visually, a line of light, a pathway, images from their past flickering below them as they travel. Others experience it entirely as sensation, a felt sense of movement, of direction, of being held above something rather than in it. Some hear things. Some simply know, without any sensory content at all, that they are there. Every experience is valid. There is no wrong way to access the Timeline, and reassuring clients of this at the start of each session is important.

What is almost universal is what happens after the release. Clients describe it as lightness — as though something heavy has been lifted without them quite noticing the moment it happened. They often report that when they try to access the emotion that brought them into the event, it is simply gone. Not suppressed, not managed — gone. The memory is still there, but the charge has left it. They can think about the experience without being in it. That distinction — between remembering and reliving — is one of the clearest markers that genuine healing has occurred rather than simply insight or relief.

And then there are the moments that stay with you as a practitioner. The client who, at forty-three, finally meets the three-year-old version of themselves who has been running the show. The person who travels to a natal experience and understands, for the first time, why they have always felt unwelcome in their own life. The moment when the learnings arise, when a client who went into an event full of shame emerges with something that sounds unmistakably like wisdom. These are the moments that remind you, session after session, why this work is different. Why going to the root matters.

— — —

The Timeline is the vehicle. The Testing Sheet is the map that tells us where to go. In the next chapter, we will explore exactly how we use the Testing Sheet to identify what is ready to be worked on, how to prioritise across sessions, and how this single document becomes the navigational tool that makes every RCT session focused, efficient, and deeply effective.

But before we move on, I want to offer you something to sit with. If you have never done Timeline work yourself, as a client, in your own healing — I encourage you to seek that experience before you begin facilitating it for others. Not because you cannot learn the technique without it, but because the felt understanding of what it is like to float above your own history, to drop into a moment from the past and finally allow it to complete, to return to the present carrying something you did not have when you left, that understanding is irreplaceable. It will change how you hold the space. It will change what you trust in a session. And it will give you a quality of presence with your clients that no amount of theoretical knowledge can substitute for.

The best practitioners of this work are those who have done it themselves. Go first. Then bring others.

Reflection

> *What is your relationship with time? Do you tend to try to leave the past in the past — or does it find its way into the present anyway? And do you let life decide your future, or do you consciously create it?*

Your reflection:

— — —

Chapter Nine: The Extended Testing Sheet

THE CENTRE FOR HEALING

Client Name:
Date Session:
Session Type/No:
Practitioner:
Soul:
Intention/Focus:

Emotions
Anger
Sadness
Fear/Anxiety
Hurt
Guilt
Shame/Ashamed
Grief/Grieving
Trauma/Abuse

Client Feedback (1-10)

Stressed	R
Anxious	R
Depressed	R
Conflict	R
Knowing Purpose	R
Personal Growth	R
Empowered	R
Peaceful	R
Mental Clarity	R
Emotional Health	R
Physical Health	R
Family	R
Relationship	R
Trusting Self	R
Spiritual Growth	R
Business/Career	R
Social Life	R
Abundance	R
Supported	R
Loved	R
Confident	R
Happy	R
Free	R
Sleep	R
Energy	R

MONITOR THOUGHTS/USAGE/BEHAVIORS PAST WEEK

Tasking/Preferences:
Future Healing:

Physical Issues:

Limiting Beliefs

I am alone	R
I am good enough	R
It is safe to be me	R
It is safe for me to relax	R
I am worthy / of love	R
I trust myself	R
I am heard	R
I can meet my own needs	R
It's safe to be vulnerable	R
I fear rejection	R
I need validation	R
I am safe in the world	R
I have enough ______	R
I fear judgement	R
Life is hard	R
I love myself	R
I trust men/women	R
I fear failure	R
Money is evil	R
I need approval	R
Safe speak my truth	R
I fear abandonment	R
I know my purpose	R
I fear conflict	R
It is safe to receive	R
I fear punishment	R
I am ashamed	R
My body is healthy	R
I am supported	R
I am confident	R
I fear success	R
I need to struggle	R
I am a rebel	R
I am loved	R
I am a ________	R
I am a ________	R
______________	R
______________	R

 V4 TCFH

The RCT Testing Sheet — the single page that holds everything a practitioner needs to see the whole person.

The Testing Sheet is not a form, it's a session guidance sheet and client results tracker.

It is a diagnostic instrument, a session map, a communication tool, and a record of healing all at once. It is the single piece of paper that holds everything a practitioner needs to see the whole person before the session begins, identify what is most ready to be worked on, track progress across the arc of the entire therapeutic relationship, and ensure that nothing important gets missed. Every section of it is deliberate. Every category was included because experience showed that leaving it out meant leaving something unaddressed that was contributing to the client's patterns.

Think of a person's life as a system of interlocking cogs. Career, relationships, physical health, sleep, finances, self-worth, family patterns, spiritual connection — each one is a cog in the mechanism, and each one is connected to the others. When one cog is out of alignment, it affects every cog it touches. A client who presents with relationship difficulties may carry physical symptoms that seem unrelated. A client whose primary complaint is chronic fatigue may have deeply held beliefs about worthiness that are quietly driving every decision they make. A sleep problem may be the most visible edge of an anxiety that has its roots in events from thirty years ago. The Testing Sheet does not allow us to look at only one cog in isolation. It holds the whole mechanism in front of us — and it is in the connections between the cogs, the places where one domain of life illuminates something in another, that the most important clinical insights are often found. Even when something seems unrelated to the presenting issue, we take note. Because in a living system, nothing is truly unrelated.

Learning to read the Testing Sheet fluently — to use it as a live document during the session rather than a static record — is one of the most important skills in Root-Cause Therapy practice. And it is what this chapter is dedicated to teaching.

Where It Begins: The Intake Form

The Testing Sheet does not begin at the first session. It begins before the client ever sits down with you.

When a client completes their intake form prior to commencing their healing journey, they are giving you a wealth of information about their history, their presenting concerns, their goals, and the patterns they are already aware of in their own life. A skilled RCT practitioner reads that intake form carefully — not just for the facts it contains, but for the picture it paints. What themes repeat? Where does the language carry the most emotional weight? What is conspicuously absent, or only mentioned in passing, that instinct suggests might be important?

From this reading, the practitioner pre-fills the Testing Sheet before the first session begins. Relevant beliefs that the intake form suggests are likely operating get marked. Emotions that are clearly present, even if not named as such — get noted.

Behaviours the client has flagged as problematic or persistent get recorded in the monitoring section. The life domain ratings will be completed with the client at the start of the session, but the practitioner arrives already oriented — not with assumptions about what the unconscious will reveal, but with a thoughtful starting point that means the session can move directly into focused, purposeful work.

This pre-filling step is one of the things that makes RCT sessions feel qualitatively different to clients from the very beginning. They do not spend the first session explaining themselves from scratch while the practitioner listens neutrally and takes notes. They arrive to find a practitioner who has already done the work of listening to what they wrote, who has questions ready, who has a sense of where to look. That experience — of being genuinely prepared for, of mattering enough that someone read what you shared and thought carefully about it — is itself therapeutic. It communicates, before a word of the session has been spoken, that this is going to be different.

> ***Practitioner Note |*** *Pre-filling is not about deciding in advance what the unconscious will reveal — it is about arriving prepared so that you can be fully present rather than orienting yourself during the session itself. Hold your pre-filled notes lightly. The sway testing process may take you in an entirely different direction, and that direction is always right. The preparation is the floor, not the ceiling.*

Session to Session: How the Testing Sheet Tracks Healing

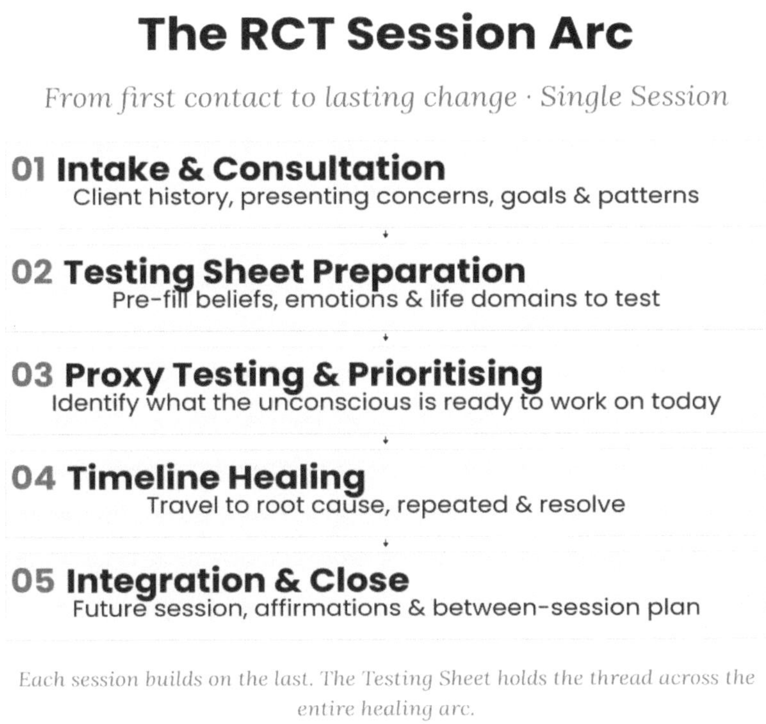

The RCT Session Arc — from intake through to integration, each step building on the last.

Each session has its own Testing Sheet. But the real power of the system is in how the sheets connect across sessions — how each one is pre-prepared from the last, creating a continuous, precise record of what has been worked on, what has shifted, and what still needs attention.

At the end of each session, before the client leaves, the practitioner reviews what was addressed and notes what remains. Beliefs that were worked on are marked. Beliefs that were identified but not yet addressed are carried forward — pre-marked on the next session's sheet so they are not forgotten and do not need to be re-identified from scratch. Emotions that partially cleared but need more work are noted. Behaviours the client has agreed to monitor in the coming week are flagged for review at the start of the next session.

When the new session begins, the practitioner already knows the landscape. They can ask with precision: how have you been feeling this week in relation to what we worked on last time? Have you noticed any changes in the beliefs we addressed? How are the behaviours you were tracking? The client is not starting over. They are continuing a journey that has clear direction, clear memory, and a practitioner who is holding the thread even between sessions.

This continuity is one of the most important things we can offer clients, particularly those who have previously experienced therapy where each session felt somewhat disconnected from the last, where they had to re-explain themselves, where nothing seemed to build. In RCT, everything builds. The Testing Sheet is the structure that makes that possible.

The Testing Sheet is not a record of what happened in a session. It is the thread that connects every session into a single, coherent journey — so that client and practitioner always know exactly where they are, where they have come from, and where they are headed next.

The Session Sequence: From Belief-Checking to Past Healing

Understanding the Testing Sheet also requires understanding the sequence it sits within because the sheet does not operate in isolation. It is the first movement in a structured session flow that takes the client from assessment to deep healing in a way that is both efficient and deeply safe.

The sequence works like this. At the start of each session, after checking in briefly with the client about their week and reviewing any significant shifts or observations, the practitioner opens the Testing Sheet and begins the sway testing process. Working through the pre-marked beliefs and any new material that has arisen, the practitioner uses the body's sway response to identify which beliefs are not currently held as true in the unconscious, which means they are active, limiting, and ready to be addressed. The emotions section is similarly checked: which emotional categories are most present and most ready to be worked on today?

Once the sway testing has identified the priority material for the session — typically one to three beliefs or emotional charges, depending on depth and what the unconscious indicates it can work with, the practitioner has everything they need to open the Timeline. The beliefs that have been identified become the focus of the past healing script. The regression begins not as a general exploration but as a targeted inquiry: what is the root cause of this specific belief, this specific emotional pattern, the first event which, when healed, will cause it to disappear?

The Testing Sheet has done its job. It has taken an entire human life — with all its complexity, all its layered history, all its intersecting patterns, and distilled it into a clear, prioritised focus for this session. The practitioner is not guessing. The client is not floundering. Both of them know exactly what they are working on and why. And the healing can proceed with a precision that simply is not possible without this level of preparation.

1. Intake form review. Practitioner reads the client's intake carefully before the first session and pre-fills the Testing Sheet with likely beliefs, relevant emotions, and behaviours to monitor.

2. Session opening. Client feedback ratings are completed together. Practitioner checks in on the previous week, any notable shifts, and anything that has arisen since the last session.

3. Sway testing. Practitioner works through the pre-marked beliefs and emotions on the Testing Sheet using the sway testing process to identify what is active and ready to be addressed today.

4. Priority identification. The one to three most relevant beliefs or emotional charges are identified as the session's focus, confirmed by the unconscious mind through sway testing.

5. Past healing script. The Timeline opens. The practitioner takes the client into the past healing regression, using the prioritised beliefs as the anchor for the root cause inquiry.

6. Session close. Learnings are integrated, the client returns fully to the present, and the practitioner notes what was addressed and pre-marks the next session's sheet before the client leaves.

> ***Practitioner Note |*** *The unconscious mind will indicate when it has had enough for a session — responses may become less clear, or the sway may stop responding as definitively. Typically up to three beliefs or root cause events per session is the natural limit. Respect this. Pushing past it does not accelerate healing — it can overwhelm the system and make integration harder. Quality over quantity, every time.*

The Testing Sheet is divided into several interconnected sections, each mapping a different dimension of the client's experience. Together they form a complete picture of where the person is right now — what they are carrying emotionally, what beliefs are operating beneath the surface, how they are experiencing their life across every significant domain, and what physical symptoms may be present.

The sections are: the session header, the client feedback ratings, the emotions, the limiting beliefs, and the physical notes. Let us walk through each in detail.

The Session Header: Intention and Orientation

The top of the Testing Sheet captures the practical details — client name, date, session number, practitioner name — but also something more important: the Soul, the Intention or Focus, and the Tasking and Preferences sections.

The Intention or Focus field is one of the most important on the entire sheet. Before any session begins, we establish clearly with the client what they want to achieve — not just in this session but in their healing overall. What do they want to feel? What would their life look like if this work went exactly as it could? This intention becomes the compass for every decision about what to prioritise.

The Tasking and Preferences field captures anything specific the client needs the practitioner to hold — sensitivities, preferences around being guided, anything from previous sessions that requires particular care. And the Future field notes anything the client is working toward or concerned about in the time ahead, which informs when future healing sessions might be appropriate and what they might focus on.

Client Feedback Ratings: The Visible Evidence of Invisible Change

The right-hand column of the Testing Sheet contains life domain ratings, a series of areas rated on a scale of one to ten, completed by the client at the start of each session based on their experience of the past week. These include emotional states such as stress, anxiety, depression, and empowerment. Relational areas — family, relationship, social life. Internal states — mental clarity, emotional health, trusting self, feeling loved, free, confident, and happy. And practical domains — business and career, financial abundance, physical health, sleep, and energy.

The ratings are taken quickly and instinctively, a gut response rather than a calculated assessment. Their power is not in any single session's numbers but in the pattern across sessions. As root causes are addressed and emotional charges cleared, these ratings shift — often dramatically, sometimes in domains the client did not expect. A client working on a core abandonment wound will frequently see their relationship and trusting self scores rise significantly, even without ever explicitly targeting those areas. The healing speaks through the data.

By sessions eight to twelve, something remarkable often happens. A client who initially struggled to articulate whether anything was changing because healing is internal and therefore initially invisible — can look at the arc of their ratings across the whole series and see, in concrete numbers, the transformation that has been occurring. Stress down from nine to two. Peace up from one to eight. Trusting self moved from three to nine. For a process that is inherently intangible, the Testing Sheet makes the evidence visible. And for clients who have struggled to trust that change is real and lasting, that visibility is profoundly affirming.

> ***Practitioner Note |*** *Review the ratings from the previous session before each new one. Notice what has shifted and what has not. Acknowledge movement explicitly — not effusively, but with honesty. "I notice your peace rating has moved from a three to a seven since we started" is a powerful moment for someone who has been in pain for a long time and may not have registered their own progress. Witnessing the arc matters as much as creating it.*

The Emotions Section: What the Body Is Carrying

The emotions section lists the primary emotional categories we work with in RCT: anger, sadness, fear and anxiety, hurt, guilt, shame, grief, and trauma or abuse. These represent the core categories that, across thousands of sessions, account for the vast majority of what clients carry and what drives their patterns.

In RCT, emotions are understood as energy in motion — or, when suppressed or interrupted, energy that has stopped moving. Every emotion on the Testing Sheet represents a process that was started by an experience and never completed. The emotion arose as a natural response to what was happening, and then something prevented it from running its full course, the environment was not safe, the person was too young, the magnitude of the event was too great to process in real time.

I often describe emotions to clients as trapped balls of energy within the body. When a trigger activates them, the energy releases stories, memories, and information — often without the conscious mind understanding why. The unresolved emotion is simultaneously trying to protect us from what hurt us and trying to attract the circumstances that will finally allow it to close the loop. In RCT, we help that process happen intentionally and safely, rather than waiting for life to keep recreating the conditions for it.

Emotions are not problems to be managed. They are processes to be completed. When we help a client finish what was interrupted, the emotion does not just reduce — it resolves. And what resolves does not return.

The Limiting Beliefs Section: The Stories Running the Show

The limiting beliefs section contains a carefully curated list of core beliefs — statements about the self and the world that, when held in the unconscious in their negative form, shape every significant decision, relationship, and pattern in a person's life.

The Level 1 Testing Sheet covers the most foundational territory: safety, worthiness, lovability, trust, identity, and connection. Beliefs such as I am good enough, I am worthy of love, it is safe to be me, I trust myself, I am heard, I am safe in the world, I know my purpose. Each of these, when the unconscious holds its inverse as true, becomes a lens through which every subsequent experience is filtered — invisible, unquestioned, and mistaken for reality.

The Extended Testing Sheet expands into specific domains: relationships, money, and the body. These are invaluable once the core Level 1 work is substantially complete and we are ready to go deeper into the patterns concentrated in particular life areas.

Crucially, we do not ask clients to consciously evaluate whether they hold these beliefs. Conscious evaluation is unreliable — most people will confidently deny beliefs that their unconscious is absolutely running. Instead, sway testing communicates directly with the unconscious mind to establish which beliefs are active and which are ready to be addressed. The Testing Sheet is the list we test from. The body provides the answers. And once the relevant beliefs are identified, they become the precise anchor for the regression that follows.

> ***Practitioner Note |*** *The beliefs are written sometimes in their negative or positive form because we are testing whether the unconscious holds them as true. When a belief tests as not true, that is what we work on. As healing progresses, beliefs that previously tested as not true will begin testing as true, a form of the arc becoming visible in the sheet itself, session by session.*

The Physical Section: The Body Keeps the Record

The physical section is brief but significant, where we note any physical symptoms or conditions the client is experiencing. Not to diagnose or treat medically, but to hold them in awareness as potential expressions of emotional or unconscious root causes.

We have seen consistently across thousands of sessions: chronic pain that resolves when its emotional root is addressed. Digestive issues that clear when a long-held anxiety imprint is released. Fatigue that lifts when suppressed grief is finally allowed to move. The body is not separate from the emotional and unconscious system — it is part of it. The Testing Sheet holds physical symptoms in the same frame as emotional ones because that is where they belong.

> ***Practitioner Note |*** *When a significant physical symptom is present, check with the unconscious mind whether addressing its emotional root is appropriate for this session. Sometimes the body is ready to bring this forward. Sometimes foundational emotional work needs to happen first. Always follow the unconscious mind's guidance on sequencing.*

Why One Sheet?

The Testing Sheet is a single page, and that is entirely deliberate. One sheet means one view, the whole person visible at a glance, without the practitioner having to move between documents or sections mid-session. Emotions, beliefs, ratings, physical notes, session intention — all present simultaneously, all available to be held in awareness at once. Pattern recognition and we can easily get a broader picture, and prioritise what to ask for in a healing.

There is something philosophically important about the constraint, too. It reminds us, every time we sit down with it, that complexity does not require complicated systems. A single page, used with skill and genuine attention, contains everything we need. The Testing Sheet is a lesson in precision — in the value of having exactly what is necessary and nothing more.

It is also one of the most compelling demonstrations of what RCT offers practitioners from backgrounds where session notes were dense, multi-page documents filled with diagnoses and treatment plans. One sheet. One session. One person, seen whole.

That is the philosophy. And as always in this work, the philosophy is where the method begins.

— — —

In the next chapter, we will explore the process that brings the Testing Sheet to life: sway testing, or muscle testing. Because identifying what is on the sheet is one thing. Knowing which of those things to work on — in what order, with what priority, confirmed by the unconscious mind itself — is something else entirely. That is where sway testing comes in. And it is one of the most fascinating and distinctive dimensions of this entire body of work.

Reflection

> *Is there a physical symptom, health pattern, or recurring theme in your life that you have never fully connected to its emotional or unconscious root? What might it be trying to tell you?*

Your reflection:

— — —

Chapter Ten: Muscle Testing

If you come from a conventional therapeutic or medical background, the idea that the body can communicate the contents of the unconscious mind through a physical movement, that you can ask someone a question and their body's sway response will tell you something true that their conscious mind may not have access to — will sound, at minimum, unusual. At maximum, it will sound like exactly the kind of claim that gives alternative approaches a poor reputation.

I understand that response completely. I had a version of it myself when I first encountered muscle testing. And I want to tell you what moved me past it — not a leap of faith, but an accumulation of evidence. Session after session, year after year, watching the sway identify root causes that the conscious mind had no access to, that led to memories and beliefs the client had not thought about in decades, that when addressed produced changes that lasted. The scepticism did not survive the evidence. And I think, if you approach this with genuine openness and try it with real clients in real sessions, yours will not either.

But let us start with the science, because the science is more solid than most people realise, and because understanding the mechanism behind sway testing is what allows you to use it with confidence rather than apology.

Why the Body Responds: The Science of Muscle Testing

Muscle testing, also known as applied kinesiology, was first developed in the 1960s by chiropractor Dr. George Goodheart[3], who observed that the strength of specific muscles changed in response to stimuli — nutritional, physical, and eventually psychological. His work was expanded by others, including Dr. John Diamond, who demonstrated that muscles weakened in response to negative stimuli and strengthened in response to positive ones — not as a deliberate, voluntary response, but as an involuntary, measurable physiological reaction.

Dr. David Hawkins took this further in his landmark work[6] on the calibration of consciousness, demonstrating through extensive research that the body's muscle response could distinguish reliably between true and false statements — between what resonated with the body's deeper intelligence and what did not. His work pointed toward something that neuroscience has since continued to confirm: the body holds information the conscious mind does not have direct access to, and it can communicate that information through involuntary physical response.

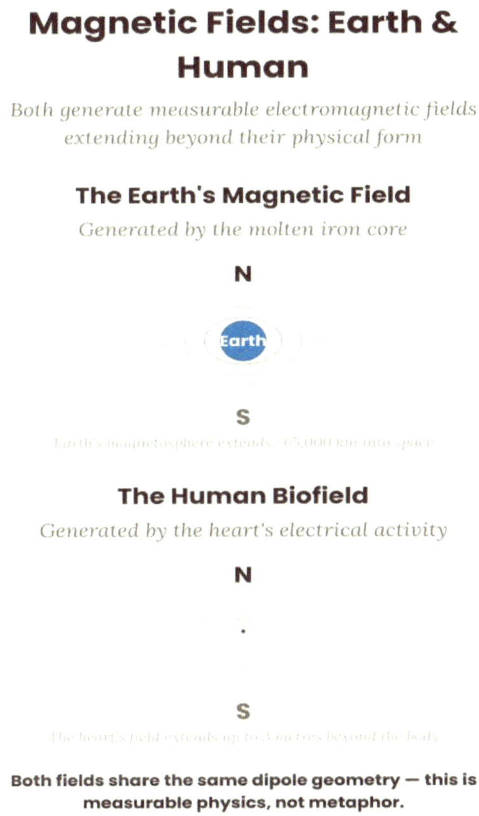

The human biofield — the body's electromagnetic field emanates forward (positive) and back (negative), providing the medium through which the sway test communicates.

What underlies all of this is the relationship between the nervous system and the unconscious mind. The unconscious mind runs the body — regulating breathing, heart rate, digestion, and hormonal response, all below the threshold of conscious awareness. It also holds every memory, belief, and emotional imprint the system has ever stored. When we ask the body a question and observe its response, we are not asking the conscious mind to evaluate the question. We are communicating directly with the system that holds all of that stored material, and the body's response reflects what that system knows, not what the thinking self has decided to believe.

This is not magic. It is physiology. The body cannot lie. The conscious mind can construct any story it needs to feel safe, with great fluency and conviction. The body simply tells the truth. And that distinction is precisely what makes sway testing so valuable in a healing context.

The conscious mind can construct any story it needs to feel safe. The body simply tells the truth. Sway testing gives us direct access to what the body knows, and what the body knows is always exactly what the healing needs.

The Sway Response: What It Is and How It Works

In Root-Cause Therapy, we use a specific form of muscle testing called the sway test, or body sway. It is the most accessible form of muscle testing — it requires no equipment, no partner, no special physical strength, and can be learned by anyone. It is also one of the most reliable, because it engages the whole body rather than a single muscle group.

The mechanics are straightforward. The person stands comfortably, feet hip-width apart, weight evenly distributed, eyes closed or softly focused. They allow the body to find its natural balance point — neither rigidly upright nor deliberately swaying, simply resting in its own equilibrium. Then a statement is made — either by the practitioner or internally by the person themselves, and the body's response is observed.

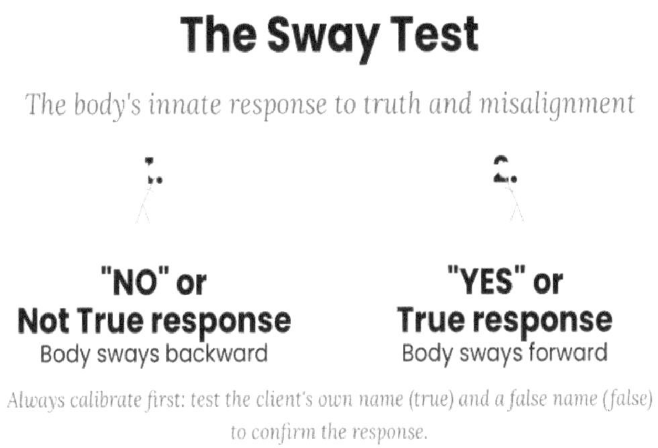

The Sway Test — a backward sway indicates a false or misaligned response; a forward sway indicates true or aligned.

A forward sway indicates a yes response, the statement is true, or resonates, or is aligned with the body's deeper knowing. A backward sway indicates a no response, the statement is false, or dissonant, or not aligned. The response is subtle in some people and quite pronounced in others. The key is that it is involuntary — not something the person is producing deliberately, but something that happens through them in response to the statement.

The first time most people experience this, they are surprised by how clearly they can feel it. There is often a moment of disbelief followed immediately by recognition, the quality of knowing something in the body before the mind has processed it. That recognition is itself significant. It is the beginning of the client's understanding that they have access to an inner intelligence more accurate and more complete than anything conscious reasoning can provide.

Calibrating the Sway: Starting With the Name

Before using the sway to test beliefs, we always calibrate it first — establishing a clear yes and a clear no so both practitioner and client know the response is working reliably for this person in this session.

The simplest calibration is the name test. Ask the client to say their own name as a statement — "My name is [name]", and observe the sway. The body should move forward. Then ask them to say a name that is not theirs. The body should sway backward. This gives both of you a concrete, unambiguous reference point for what yes and no look like in this person's body.

A note on names that matters: not everyone identifies most strongly with their legal name. Some clients go by a nickname, a middle name, or a name they have given themselves that carries more personal resonance than the name on their intake form. If the calibration does not produce a clear forward sway on the name you have used, try alternatives. The name that produces the strongest forward sway is the one to use — it is the name the unconscious most closely associates with the self.

A note on identity that is equally important: when calibrating with identity-based statements, be conscious of the language you use and who is in the room. Statements like "I am a woman" or "I am a man" may not resonate clearly for non-binary or gender-diverse clients, and using them without awareness can inadvertently create dissonance in the testing process, and more importantly, can communicate to the client that the practitioner has made assumptions about who they are. For clients whose gender identity is relevant to the calibration, ask them how they would prefer to be referred to and use that language. The sway tests the client's truth, not our assumptions.

> ***Practitioner Note |*** *Calibration is not a box to tick quickly before the real work. It is the foundation of everything that follows. Take the time to get a clear, reliable yes and no established before you move to the beliefs. A session built on an uncalibrated sway is a session built on uncertain ground.*

Self-Testing: Giving Clients Access to Their Own Knowing

One of the things I value most about sway testing is that it is not only a tool for the practitioner. It is a tool we can teach clients to use for themselves, and doing so is one of the most genuinely empowering things we can offer in the context of a healing relationship.

When a client learns to sway test their own beliefs between sessions, something important shifts. They are no longer dependent on the practitioner to tell them what is true for them. They have direct access to the same system we are working with in sessions — their own unconscious intelligence, and they can consult it about anything. Is this belief still active? Does this decision feel aligned for me? Is this emotion present and ready to be acknowledged?

This builds the client's relationship with their own body in a way that extends far beyond the therapeutic context. Many people who come to RCT have spent years overriding their body's signals — numbing what was uncomfortable, rationalising what felt wrong, staying in situations the body was clearly telling them to leave. Teaching them to listen through sway testing is not just a clinical technique. It is the beginning of a fundamentally different relationship with their own inner knowing.

> ***Practitioner Note |*** *Teach clients to frame sway test questions as clear, present-tense statements rather than open questions. "I am safe" rather than "Am I safe?" "This decision is right for me" rather than "Is this right?" The body responds more reliably to declarative statements, which bypass the analytical mind and allow the unconscious to respond without interference.*

How Sway Testing Works in an RCT Session

In the context of an RCT session, sway testing is the bridge between the Testing Sheet and the Timeline. It takes the list of potential beliefs and emotions on the sheet and identifies, with precision, which ones are active in the unconscious right now, which are most ready to be worked on today, and in what order to approach them.

For each belief on the Testing Sheet, the statement is read in its positive form — "I am good enough," "It is safe to be me," "I am worthy of love." A forward sway means the unconscious holds this as true. A backward sway means the limiting belief is active and is a candidate for the session's focus. From the beliefs that test as not true, the practitioner identifies, again through sway testing, which one or two are most ready and most important to address today.

Once the priority beliefs have been identified, the session moves into the past healing script. The beliefs become the anchor for the root cause inquiry on the Timeline. The sway has done its work — it has told us exactly where to go, confirmed by the client's own body. The deeper healing can now proceed with complete clarity about what it is working on and why.

A note on the specificity of beliefs: if the sway produces a wobbling or uncertain response to a particular belief — swaying neither clearly forward nor clearly backward. This is usually a signal that the belief needs to be made more specific for this client. A wobble is the body's way of saying yes and no simultaneously, which typically means the statement is partially true and partially not. For example, "I am worthy" might produce a wobble for a client who feels worthy in some areas of life but not others. Adjusting to "I am worthy of love" or "I am worthy of financial abundance" — something more precise — will often produce a clearer response. As you get to know your clients, you will develop a feel for how to fine-tune the language of beliefs to match their specific experience.

What the Body Knows That the Mind Doesn't

The conscious mind is a magnificent editor. It constructs coherent, self-consistent narratives about who we are and why we do what we do — so fluently that most of us experience those narratives as simply true. We believe our own story.

The sway test cuts through the edited version. When a client says with complete conviction "I know I am worthy — I have done so much work on this," and the body sways backward on "I am worthy of love," that discrepancy is not a failure of self-awareness. It is the difference between what the conscious mind has been told and what the unconscious mind still holds as true. The work of self-development has reached the surface. The root has not yet been cleared.

I have seen this play out in ways that still move me, even after thousands of sessions. A client who has been in personal development for years, who can articulate their wounds with sophisticated clarity — whose body sways backward on "I am loved" with the same quiet certainty as someone who has never reflected on themselves a day in their life. The body does not grade on effort. It reports what is true. And once we know exactly where the unconscious is still holding the old story, we know exactly where to go.

— — —

Troubleshooting the Sway: When It Doesn't Work as Expected

Every practitioner, however experienced, encounters sessions where the sway response is unclear, inconsistent, or absent. This is not a failure of the method — it is feedback. Something in the system is asking for attention before the deeper work can proceed. Here is what to look for and what to do.

The body is not moving at all

A completely still body usually indicates one of a few things. The most common is stress or anxiety, when the nervous system is in a heightened state, the body can lock up rather than respond freely. Ask the client to pause, close their eyes, and take several slow, deep breaths into the belly. Give this a full minute rather than a few seconds. The nervous system needs time to downshift.

Dehydration is the other frequent culprit and is more common than most practitioners expect. The body's electrical conductivity, which underlies the sway response, is significantly affected by hydration. If breathing and grounding do not produce a response, ask the client to drink a full glass of water before continuing. You can also gently place your hands on the client's lower back over the kidneys and hold for a moment, which can help activate the body's hydration response. And check yourself, the practitioner's own hydration matters too. If you are dehydrated, your ability to hold a clear energetic space for the testing is compromised.

Grounding is the third factor to check. Ask the client to feel their feet on the floor — really feel them, the weight, the contact, the solidity of the ground beneath them. Some practitioners find it helpful to invite clients to imagine roots extending from their feet down into the earth. When a person is not grounded, the sway can be sluggish or absent. When they are grounded, it tends to become immediate and clear.

> ***Practitioner Note |*** *In early sessions, particularly the first two or three, clients may not produce large visible sway movements even when the response is present. The body is still learning to communicate this way, and the movements can be very subtle, a slight lean, a barely perceptible shift in weight. If this is the case, ask the client to verbalise what they are feeling internally: a pull forward, a push back, a feeling of resistance or openness. Their internal experience is valid information even when the external movement is not yet pronounced. With practice across sessions, the response almost always becomes clearer and more visible.*

The sway is reversed — forward for no, backward for yes

Occasionally, a client's magnetic field is switched, meaning their body's polarity is running in the opposite direction from usual. This produces a sway that appears backward — they move forward on statements that should produce a no, and backward on statements that should produce a yes. You will notice this during calibration if the body sways backward on their own name.

To correct this, use your hands and intention to turn their magnetic field around. Working with your hands around the client's body — not touching, but moving through the energetic field — imagine reorienting the field so that the positive pole is in front of them and the negative pole is behind, as it should be. Think of it like reorienting a battery that has been placed in the wrong direction, or like the magnetic field of the earth — we have one too, and it can temporarily become misaligned. Once corrected, re-calibrate with the name test before continuing.

Another simple technique: ask the client to sway deliberately forward while saying "yes, yes, yes" and then deliberately backward while saying "no, no, no." Doing this several times helps the body anchor the correct direction for each response and can reset a switched or confused pattern quickly.

The sway is wobbling rather than moving clearly in one direction

A wobble, the body swaying neither clearly forward nor clearly backward, or oscillating between the two — is the body's way of communicating ambivalence. It is a yes and a no simultaneously, which typically means the belief as stated is too broad or too generalised for this client's specific experience.

When you encounter a wobble, adjust the belief to be more specific. "I am worthy" might wobble for someone who feels worthy in relationships but not in their career — try "I am worthy of success" or "I am worthy of financial abundance" to get a cleaner response. As you build your knowledge of a client across sessions, you will develop an instinct for how to tune the language of each belief to match their particular pattern. A more specific belief will almost always produce a clearer answer from the body.

The client speaks English as a second language

If the sway is slow to respond or appears confused for a client whose first language is not English, this is often because the body is translating the belief internally before it can respond, and that translation takes time and mental energy that can interfere with the somatic response. Before beginning the testing, show the client the Testing Sheet and give them a moment to read through the beliefs quietly, allowing them to translate internally at their own pace. Be patient with the response time. The sway will come — it simply needs more space to arrive. You can also invite the client to hold the belief in their first language internally while you read it in English, which can produce a clearer and faster response.

The client's analytical mind keeps interfering

Some clients, particularly those who are very intellectually oriented or who have been trained in disciplines that emphasise critical thinking — find it difficult to allow the sway to happen without the mind jumping in to evaluate, predict, or control the response. They are trying to get the right answer rather than allowing the body's answer to arise.

When this happens, invite the client to soften their focus — to look at a point on the floor rather than closing their eyes tightly, to breathe through the mouth gently, to imagine they are simply an observer of whatever the body does. You can also ask them to say the belief out loud rather than thinking it, which can shift the locus of processing from the analytical mind to the somatic system. With practice and reassurance across sessions, most analytically oriented clients find that their sway becomes easier to access as they build trust in the process.

Nothing is working, the sway is simply not accessible for this client

In rare cases, after trying all of the above, a client may simply not be able to access a reliable sway response. This is not a limitation of their capacity to heal — it is a communication from the body that a different form of testing will work better for them.

The first alternative is the hand pendulum, a simple pendulum held between thumb and forefinger, which moves in response to the same energetic signals that produce the body sway. Forward or circular movement indicates yes; backward or opposite movement indicates no. Many clients who cannot produce a clear body sway can access a reliable pendulum response quite readily.

The second alternative is finger lock testing, a form of muscle testing where the client creates a circle with their thumb and forefinger and the practitioner attempts to pull it open while the client resists. A strong hold indicates yes; the fingers pulling apart easily indicates no. This is particularly useful for clients who cannot stand comfortably or who have physical limitations that make body sway impractical.

A third option — surrogate testing, where the practitioner muscle tests themselves on behalf of the client — is available but is not recommended for practitioners who are early in their practice. It requires a level of energetic clarity and skill that develops with experience, and until that foundation is solid, the results are not reliable enough to build a session on.

> ***Practitioner Note |*** *Whatever testing method you use, always re-calibrate before the session's substantive work begins. A clear yes and a clear no, reliably established, is the non-negotiable foundation. Without it, you are guessing, and your clients deserve better than that.*

A note on a distinction that is easy to conflate but important to keep separate. If a client is not producing a sway response, the reason may not be any of the physical or energetic factors above. It may be that their nervous system is in a state of hyperactivation — too flooded, too on-edge, too braced — to allow even subtle body movement. In this case, the priority is not to find a different testing method. It is to slow everything down, breathe together, help the person feel genuinely safe in the room, and let the session wait until the nervous system has come down enough to participate. You cannot heal a nervous system that does not yet feel safe enough to be present. Regulation always comes before technique.

A separate and equally important distinction: some clients cannot access visual imagery at all, a condition known as aphantasia, or mind-blindness. This is relevant not just for sway testing but for the regression work that follows, and we have a dedicated script for working with aphantasic clients. The key is to shift from picture-based language to body-based and sensation-based language throughout. Rather than asking "What do you see?" ask "What do you notice in your body?" or "What does it feel like?" or "If that had a sensation, what would it be?" Many clients access memory, belief, and emotional charge entirely through feeling rather than imagery, and that is completely valid. The healing is not in the picture. It is in the somatic release. Images are simply one pathway there, and not the only one.

> **Practitioner Note |** *If you find yourself becoming anxious because the sway is not working, notice that. Your*

> *anxiety will amplify the block rather than resolve it. The client's nervous system is exquisitely sensitive to the practitioner's state — if you are tense or frustrated, they will feel it and contract further. Your most powerful tool in any moment of difficulty is your own regulation. Breathe. Slow down. Remember that you are not forcing a response — you are creating the conditions for one. Sometimes the most therapeutic thing you can do is simply be calm and unhurried while the body finds its way to safety. The sway will come when the system is ready. Trust that.*

— — —

An Invitation to Try It Before You Judge It

I want to close this chapter with something I say to every cohort of new practitioners at the beginning of their training, because I think it is the most useful frame for approaching sway testing, and for approaching everything in this body of work that sits at the edge of what conventional training has prepared you for.

Do not decide in advance. Try it first.

Not in a session with a client — not until you have practised and developed confidence. But with yourself, with a trusted colleague, with a willing friend. Calibrate it. Play with it. Ask it things you already know the answer to and observe whether the body confirms them. Notice what happens when you ask it something you have been avoiding knowing.

What almost everyone discovers is that the sway is not strange. It is familiar. It is the gut feeling that turned out to be right. The sense of wrongness that preceded a decision you later regretted. The inexplicable resistance your body has sometimes had to things your mind was trying to convince you were fine. We have all been receiving this communication from the body our entire lives. Sway testing simply gives it a structure, a way of asking directly and listening clearly, rather than hoping we notice the signal amid the noise.

When you experience that recognition, and I believe you will, the question of whether it is real will dissolve. Not because you decided to believe in it, but because you felt it in your own body. And felt understanding, as we have established throughout this book, is the only kind that actually changes anything.

In the next chapter, we turn to limiting beliefs, the specific beliefs that sway testing most commonly identifies, why they form, how they operate, and what happens in a person's life and nervous system when they are finally released at the root.

Reflection

Your reflection:

Chapter Eleven: Limiting Beliefs

What I know, and what I am quietly holding while they speak — is that what they are describing is not the world. It is their map of the world. And the map, in this case, was drawn a very long time ago, by a very young person, in response to experiences that were real and painful and entirely formative. The map made sense then. It was, in fact, an act of intelligence, a child's nervous system doing precisely what it needed to do to navigate what it was experiencing. The tragedy is only that the map has never been updated. And a person navigating an adult life with a childhood map will keep arriving at destinations they did not choose, wondering why the territory never seems to match what they hoped for.

That childhood map is made of limiting beliefs. And this chapter is about what they are, how they form, what they cost us, and what becomes possible when they are finally released at the root.

What a Limiting Belief Actually Is

A limiting belief is not simply a negative thought. This distinction matters, because if we treat limiting beliefs as thoughts — as cognitive content that can be addressed by substituting better thoughts — we will always be working at the wrong level. Thoughts are the surface. Beliefs are the structure beneath them.

A belief is a conclusion the unconscious mind has drawn from experience and encoded as truth. It is not evaluated or held lightly, the way an opinion is. It is operated from, the way a foundation is operated from. The house does not think about its foundation. It simply rests on it, and everything about its structure reflects it. Limiting beliefs function in exactly this way. They are the unconscious premises from which the entire architecture of a person's inner life is built.

And because they operate at the level of the unconscious — below language, below deliberate thought, below the reach of most conventional therapeutic approaches — they are extraordinarily resistant to change through the methods that work at the conscious level. Affirmations do not shift them. Cognitive reframing does not dissolve them. Insight, however accurate, does not touch them. They change when the experience that created them is healed — not described, not understood, not reframed, but healed. At the root.

What makes limiting beliefs so consequential is not just that they produce negative thoughts. It is that they narrow everything. They contract the field of what a person can perceive, what they consider possible, what they allow themselves to want and to reach for and to receive. A belief shapes not just how we see ourselves — it shapes how we see the world. It determines what we notice and what we overlook, which opportunities register as real and which feel inaccessible before we have even consciously evaluated them. It makes us rigid where we could be open, defended where we could be receptive, contracted where we could expand.

A person living from the belief I am not enough will not simply think negative thoughts about themselves. They will filter every piece of feedback through that lens, unconsciously discounting the evidence that contradicts it and amplifying the evidence that confirms it. They will shrink in rooms where they could lead. They will stay in relationships that reflect the belief back to them, because relationships that offer genuine love and appreciation will feel unfamiliar, even threatening — to a nervous system that has organised itself around not-enoughness as its baseline reality.

This is what we mean when we say a belief is limiting. It does not just limit what we think. It limits what we can see, what we can receive, and ultimately what becomes possible in our life.

A belief is not just a thought we have. It is the lens through which we see everything. Change the lens, and the entire world looks different — not because the world changed, but because we can finally see what was always there.

How Limiting Beliefs Form

Dr. Bruce Lipton's research in the biology of belief[5] offers one of the most illuminating accounts of how our core beliefs are installed, and why they are so difficult to shift through conscious effort alone.

Lipton's work demonstrated that children between birth and approximately seven years of age operate primarily in theta and delta brainwave states, the same states associated in adults with hypnosis and deep meditation. In these states, the mind is extraordinarily receptive. It absorbs experience without the critical filtering that the adult conscious mind applies. Everything that happens — everything that is witnessed, everything that is felt, every conclusion that is drawn about the self and the world — goes directly into the programming of the unconscious mind, bypassing any capacity for evaluation or questioning.

This is why the beliefs formed in childhood are so foundational and so persistent. They were not chosen. They were not evaluated. They were simply absorbed — from what we experienced, from what we were told, from what we watched the adults around us do and believe and suffer through. And once encoded, they operate as fact — not as one possible interpretation of the world, but as the world itself.

How a Limiting Belief Is Formed

The pathway from an event to an encoded belief held in the body

Event
A moment of overwhelming experience

Perception
The meaning the system assigns in that moment

Emotion
The emotional charge that arises from it

Thought
The conclusion formed while in the feeling

Belief
Encoded as truth in the nervous system

RCT heals by returning to the root event — completing what was left unfinished

The process happens automatically, outside conscious awareness, as moments the nervous system experiences as overwhelming.

The pathway from event to encoded belief — perception shapes emotion, which generates the thought, which becomes the belief held in the body.

A child who grows up witnessing a parent be repeatedly let down by people they love does not consciously decide that people cannot be trusted. The belief forms below the threshold of decision. It simply becomes part of how things are, a quiet certainty, carried forward into every subsequent relationship, shaping every choice about who to let close and how far.

A child who is praised only when they perform, who never quite receives approval simply for existing, does not choose to believe that love is conditional on achievement. The belief is the conclusion the nervous system draws from the accumulated pattern of experience, and it runs forward into adulthood as the invisible operating system behind every striving, every overgiving, every difficulty with receiving without earning.

This is not blame. The parents and caregivers who were the environment in which these beliefs formed were almost always doing their best with what they themselves had been given. Limiting beliefs pass down through families not through malice but through unhealed experience — each generation transmitting to the next the unconscious conclusions they drew from their own wounds. The cycle continues until someone heals it.

That is what we are doing in Root-Cause Therapy. We are finding the moment the belief was formed, the specific, often long-forgotten event where the unconscious drew its conclusion, and we are going there. Not to revisit it as a story, but to heal it as an experience. To complete what was incomplete. And in doing so, to update the programming at the level where it was originally installed.

When the Belief Changes, the World Changes

I want to share something personal here, because I think it illustrates more clearly than any theoretical explanation what it actually means for a limiting belief to shift — not just cognitively, but at the level of perception and possibility.

For a significant part of my adult life, I carried a belief that I did not consciously hold but that the sway would have identified immediately: I don't trust men.

It made complete sense in the context of what I had grown up witnessing. Domestic violence. Abuse. The pattern of men in my early environment being sources of danger, unpredictability, or abandonment rather than safety and care. My nervous system drew the only reasonable conclusion available to it: men are not safe. Men cannot be trusted. And that conclusion, encoded before I had any capacity to question it, became the filter through which I encountered every man I subsequently met.

The consequence was not that I consciously avoided men or told myself negative things about them. The consequence was subtler and more total than that. I kept attracting men I couldn't trust deeply — not because I was choosing poorly in any deliberate sense, but because the belief was doing the choosing for me. It was filtering out the evidence that contradicted it and drawing toward me the experiences that confirmed it. A nervous system organised around the belief that men cannot be trusted will, without any conscious intention, find the men who prove that belief right. Not always. But with a consistency that feels, from the inside, like fate.

When I finally addressed this belief at the root, when we found the original experiences that had generated it and completed the healing of those moments — something changed that I had not anticipated. It was not that I simply thought differently about men. It was that I could suddenly see differently. Men I might previously have overlooked or dismissed registered to me as genuinely safe. Trustworthy. Present. The evidence that had always been there, that the belief had been filtering out, became visible.

And it was from that changed perception, that opened, updated, no-longer-contracted way of seeing, that I was able to recognise and receive the person who became my partner, the co-founder of The Centre for Healing, and the father of my child. He did not appear after the belief shifted as though conjured from nowhere. He was simply finally visible to me. The belief had not been keeping men away. It had been keeping me from being able to see what was already there.

That is what a limiting belief does when it is present. And that is what becomes possible when it is gone.

— — —

The Core Categories of Limiting Beliefs

The beliefs we work with in Root-Cause Therapy are not random. They reflect the core domains of human experience where unconscious programming most profoundly shapes the quality of a person's life. Understanding these categories, and the way beliefs within each category tend to cluster and compound — is essential for using the Testing Sheet with real depth.

The most foundational beliefs are those of safety and identity — beliefs about whether it is safe to exist as oneself, whether one is inherently worthy, whether one can be trusted and can trust oneself. Beliefs such as it is safe to be me, I am good enough, I trust myself, I am worthy of love. These are the deepest layer of the programming because they were often formed earliest, and because everything else rests on them. A person who does not believe at the unconscious level that it is safe to be themselves will struggle in every domain — relationships, career, creativity, health because the foundational operating system is running a programme of contraction and concealment that touches everything.

The relational beliefs sit just above this layer — beliefs about what love is and how it behaves, about abandonment and connection, about whether it is safe to be seen and known by another person. Relationships lead to pain. Love is meant to feel stressful or unsafe. I always get abandoned. I am always betrayed. It is safe for me to be loved. These beliefs are often formed in the context of early attachment relationships — with parents, caregivers, siblings, and they replay with extraordinary fidelity in every significant adult relationship until the root is addressed.

The beliefs around worth and money reflect the unconscious conclusions drawn about one's right to take up space, to receive, to be compensated, to have more than one was given. I have to struggle to be wealthy. I am worthy of financial abundance. Rich people are bad. It is safe for me to have more than my family. These beliefs are among the most practically consequential in a client's life, and they are among the most satisfying to address because the changes they produce in a person's external circumstances can be rapid and unmistakable once the root is cleared.

The beliefs about the body are often the most intimate and the most painful — I am ashamed of my body, I need to be a certain way to be safe, food protects me, it serves me to have an illness. These beliefs are particularly important to approach with care and without assumption. A body belief is often carrying the weight of experiences the conscious mind has never fully acknowledged — violation, neglect, the chronic experience of the body as a source of shame or danger rather than home. The healing of body beliefs can be among the most profound and tender work in this entire practice.

> ***Practitioner Note |*** *When working with body-related beliefs, slow down more than you think you need to. The body has often been the site of the wound itself — not just the carrier of the emotional charge but the actual location where something happened. Approach this territory with particular gentleness, ensure the client feels completely safe before going anywhere near the root, and follow the unconscious mind's guidance carefully about what is ready to be addressed and in what sequence.*

Why Beliefs Are So Hard to Shift: The Role of Emotion and Trauma

Here is something that is essential to understand, and that most approaches to belief change miss entirely: a limiting belief does not exist in isolation. It is held in place by emotion. Specifically, by the unprocessed emotional charge of the experience that created it, and in many cases, by the weight of trauma that made that emotion too overwhelming to feel at the time it arose.

Think of it this way. When something happens to a young person that is too much, too fast, or too frightening to process, when there is no safe adult present to help them metabolise what they are feeling, no language for the experience, no permission to express what is arising, the nervous system does something intelligent and automatic. It freezes the emotion in place. It locks the feeling down, buries it beneath the threshold of conscious awareness, and builds a belief around it like a wall. The belief — I am not safe, I am not enough, I cannot trust — is not just a conclusion. It is a protective structure. It exists to keep the person from having to feel the unbearable thing that is stored beneath it.

This is why affirmations do not work for deeply held limiting beliefs. It is why telling yourself a different story does not shift them. It is why a person can consciously believe, with complete sincerity, that they are worthy, and still find themselves acting from unworthiness in every area that truly matters. The conscious mind has adopted the new narrative.

But the emotional charge beneath the old belief is still present, still locked in the body, still running the system from below. And as long as that charge remains, the belief remains because the belief is the nervous system's way of making sure we never have to feel what is underneath it.

This is particularly true for beliefs formed in childhood, because the emotional experiences of childhood are the ones we are least equipped to process. A child does not have the neurological development, the emotional vocabulary, the relational support, or the life experience to metabolise what a significant trauma or a pattern of chronic adversity produces in the body. The feelings are too large for the container. So the container locks them away. And the belief forms over the top, like scar tissue — functional, protective, and completely invisible to the person living inside it.

Without something that works at the root — without a method that can go to where the emotional charge is actually stored and help the nervous system finally complete what was interrupted — these beliefs do not resolve on their own. Time does not heal them. Understanding does not dissolve them. A person can spend decades in personal development, reading every book, attending every workshop, intellectually grasping every insight, and still find themselves, at fifty or sixty or seventy, living from the same unconscious conclusions they drew at five. Still believing, somewhere beneath everything they know, that they are not quite enough. That they do not quite deserve it. That failure is the most likely outcome, so it is safer not to try.

And this is where the cost becomes real. Because a limiting belief carried unhealed through an entire life is not just a negative thought pattern. It is a life unlived. It is the career never pursued because the fear of failure felt too certain. The relationship never fully entered because the belief that love leads to pain kept one foot always near the door. The dream quietly abandoned because the belief I am not enough arrived before the attempt and made the outcome feel inevitable. The person who spends their whole life believing they are not worthy of abundance, and dies never having allowed themselves to truly receive it — not because it was not available, but because the belief made them unable to see it, unable to reach for it, unable to let it in.

This is what is at stake in this work. Not just symptom relief. Not just feeling a little better. The full reclamation of a life that the wound was quietly stealing, one unlived moment at a time.

A limiting belief carried unhealed is not just a thought pattern. It is a life that keeps contracting, the dream not pursued, the love not fully entered, the potential not reached because somewhere beneath everything, the wound is still saying: it is not safe, you are not enough, do not try.

When we heal the emotional root of a limiting belief, when we allow the nervous system to finally complete what was interrupted, to feel what was frozen, to release what has been locked in the body, sometimes for decades, the belief does not just soften. It loses its reason to exist. And what floods in to fill the space is not a manufactured positive thought. It is the person's actual truth. The one that was always there beneath the wound, waiting for the weight of it to lift.

That is what Root-Cause Therapy makes possible. Not the replacement of one belief with another. The clearing of the emotional charge that was holding the limiting belief in place — so that what remains is not a new story, but an absence of the old one, and the freedom that absence creates.

— — —

What Shifts When a Belief Is Released

I want to be precise about what actually happens when a limiting belief is released through RCT, because the language of belief change can easily become vague, and this process is anything but.

When we take a client to the root cause of a limiting belief, when they access the original event, release the emotional charge that has been stored there, receive the learnings, and return to the present along the Timeline — several things happen simultaneously. The memory remains, but the charge leaves it. The client can recall what happened without being pulled back into the feeling of it. The past becomes the past rather than an ongoing present-tense experience.

The belief itself — I don't trust men, I am not enough, I am not worthy of love — loses what I can only describe as its grip. Not because it has been argued away or replaced with a more positive version of itself, but because the experience that generated it has been completed. The unconscious no longer needs to hold the conclusion, because the wound that produced it has been healed. The belief was never the problem. It was the nervous system's faithful response to the problem. Heal the wound, and the response resolves naturally.

What follows is not always immediately visible. Sometimes clients notice changes within hours of a session, a lightness, a different quality of attention, a reaction that simply does not arise where it always did before. Sometimes the shifts become apparent over the days and weeks that follow, as the nervous system integrates what was released and the new programming begins to express itself in behaviour and perception. Sometimes a client cannot quite name what has changed — only that something has. That the room feels different. That they responded differently to something that usually triggered them. That they found themselves making a choice they could not have made before.

And sometimes — not always, but often enough that it has ceased to surprise me, the change announces itself through what arrives in a person's life. The relationship that becomes possible when the belief that blocked it has cleared. The opportunity that was always there but invisible until the narrowed perception opened. The version of themselves they catch a glimpse of in the mirror and recognise, perhaps for the first time, as genuinely their own.

— — —

Reflection

> *What is the belief about yourself that has cost you the most? Not the one that's easiest to name — the one you sense is quietly running the show.*

Your reflection:

— — —

Chapter Twelve: The RCT Session in Practice

The best sessions happen when the practitioner knows the structure so well they no longer need to think about it. When the sequence is in the body rather than the head. When every question arises from genuine presence and genuine curiosity rather than from following a checklist. That fluency comes with practice. This chapter gives you the map. The practice will give you everything else.

Before the Session Begins

The session begins before the client arrives. It begins with you.

Review the Testing Sheet from the previous session — or, for a new client, the intake form you have used to pre-fill the first sheet. Know what you are working with. Know what was addressed last time and what remains. Know the intention the client has set for their healing overall, and hold it as the quiet compass for everything that follows.

Attend to your own state. This is not a minor point. The practitioner's nervous system is not a neutral bystander in the session — it is part of the field in which the healing happens. A regulated, grounded, genuinely present practitioner creates conditions in which the client's nervous system can settle. A stressed or distracted or unresourced practitioner creates the opposite, and no amount of technical skill compensates for it. Take whatever time you need — five minutes of stillness, a few conscious breaths, whatever helps you arrive fully — so that when your client walks in, they are met by someone who is genuinely there.

Make sure you are hydrated. Make sure the space is comfortable, private, and free from interruption. And hold, somewhere quietly in your awareness, the essential truth about the person who is about to sit across from you: they are not broken. They are whole beneath what they are carrying. Your job is not to fix them. It is to help them find their way back to what was always there.

> ***Practitioner Note |*** *Your own healing is the foundation of your practice. The more of your own root-cause work you have done, the more regulated and present you will be able to be with your clients' pain. You cannot hold space beyond the edge of your own healing. This is not a criticism or saying that you aren't good enough, as the training has been created even for a beginner person—but it is an invitation to keep going in your own work, continuously, as a practitioner. The two journeys are not separate.*

Stage 1 Opening and Check-In

Begin by welcoming the client and giving them a moment to settle. For returning clients, open with a genuine check-in:

how have they been since last session? What did they notice in the days that followed the previous healing? What has shifted, however subtly, and what feels the same or has felt harder?

This opening conversation is not small talk. It is diagnostic. The client's account of their week tells you how the previous session is integrating, which beliefs are continuing to shift and which may need more work, and what is most alive and present for them right now. Listen not just to the content but to the body, where their energy is, what lights up as they speak, where the flatness or the heaviness or the activation lives.

For a new client, use this opening to establish rapport and safety before anything else. Ask them what brought them here. Listen to how they describe their experience, the language they reach for, the themes that recur, the things they say and the things they stop just short of saying. All of it is information. None of it is wasted.

At the end of the check-in, invite the client to complete the feedback ratings on the Testing Sheet, the life domain scores for the past week. Do this together, conversationally rather than administratively. As they give you each number, a brief acknowledgement — "okay, a four on peace this week, got it" — keeps the energy moving and builds a natural rhythm between you before the deeper work begins.

> ***Practitioner Note |*** *Do not rush the opening. New practitioners often feel an urgency to get to the "real" work, the testing, the Timeline, the regression. But the opening is real work. A client who does not yet feel safe in the room, or who has not yet felt genuinely heard, will not be able to access the depth of unconscious material that the session requires. Safety is not a precondition to the session. It is the first thing you build, actively and intentionally, every time.*

Stage 2 Sway Testing and Priority Identification

Once the opening is complete and the ratings are recorded, the session moves into sway testing. Invite the client to stand, orient them to the process — or for returning clients, simply reconnect them to it with a brief reminder, and begin calibration.

Establish a clear yes and a clear no using the name test before moving to any belief content. Once the calibration is solid, begin working through the pre-marked beliefs on the Testing Sheet. Read each one in its positive form, observe the body's response, and note the result. Move through the list with a calm, steady pace — not rushed, not hesitant. The rhythm of the testing helps the client stay relaxed and responsive rather than tightening into analysis.

As the testing proceeds, you will notice which beliefs produce a clear backward sway, the ones the unconscious does not currently hold as true. These are your candidates for the session's focus. Once you have identified the active beliefs, use the sway to confirm which one or two are most ready and most important to work on today. Ask directly: is [belief] the most important thing to address in this session? Follow the body's guidance rather than your own clinical instinct about what seems most significant. The unconscious knows the sequencing better than we do.

Note the priority beliefs clearly on the Testing Sheet. These become the anchor for the regression that follows.

> ***Practitioner Note |*** *Some clients find the transition from seated check-in to standing for sway testing slightly abrupt if it is not bridged well. A simple sentence — "Now I'd like us to do some belief testing, which will tell us exactly what to focus on today. Can I ask you to stand for me?" — is enough. The clearer and more confident your invitation, the more easily the client follows. Hesitation in the practitioner produces hesitation in the client.*

Stage 3 Opening the Timeline

With the priority beliefs identified, invite the client to close their eyes and begin the process of relaxation and orientation to the Timeline. Use a gentle, lowered voice — speaking slightly more slowly and softly than in normal conversation, allowing the tone itself to begin the shift from conscious engagement to unconscious access.

Guide the client through a brief body relaxation — noticing any tension, releasing on each exhale, relaxing the forehead and the jaw, allowing the body to sink deeper into the chair or the floor. Then ask the unconscious mind where the past is, and where the future is — inviting the client to point without thinking, trusting the first impulse.

For a first session, take time to map the full Timeline — floating out to the far past, noticing what is there, floating to the far future, noticing what is there, returning to now, and then floating higher until the entire Timeline is visible as a small line below. This full mapping only needs to happen once. In subsequent sessions, you can move directly to the working position above the present moment.

Once the client is oriented above the Timeline, turn them toward the past and prepare for the first question of the healing.

> ***Practitioner Note |*** *Underline your voice when speaking to the unconscious mind. This is not an affectation — it is a deliberate technique. A slightly lower, slower vocal register speaks more directly to the unconscious mind, partially bypassing the critical conscious filter. You will notice, when you find the right register, that clients' responses become more immediate and more embodied. The voice is one of your most important instruments. Use it with intention.*

Stage 4 The Past Healing: Going to the Root

With the client above their Timeline and facing the past, begin the root cause inquiry. First, confirm with the unconscious mind that it is willing and ready to release this belief or emotion today, and that the client can be aware of it consciously. If the answer is yes, proceed. If no, reassure gently — "you are completely safe, we are going there for the purpose of healing, not reliving", and try again. If the unconscious consistently declines on a particular belief, trust that and move to the next one on the list.

Ask the first root cause question: what is the root cause of this problem, the first event, which when healed will cause the problem to disappear? Was it before, during, or after birth?

Note the answer and follow with the age or timing — how old were they, how many generations ago, how many months before birth. Then ask the unconscious mind to float up above the Timeline, travel to that point, and drop all the way down into the event — so the client is looking through their own eyes, present in the experience, feeling what was felt there.

Once they are in the event, ask what is happening. What emotions or sensations are present? Where are they felt in the body? How intense, on a scale of zero to ten? And then, when the client is ready, and with clear permission — guide them into the release. Turn the emotion up like a volume dial, all the way to its peak, holding steady as the charge moves. Stay present. Stay calm. Your steadiness is the container.

When the emotion begins to come down, and it will, because emotions that are fully allowed always complete — guide the client through slow deep breaths to help the energy move and dissipate. Wait until the charge has fully cleared before moving on. A partial release is not a complete one. Check: is there anything else? Any other emotion or sensation still present? Repeat the process for each layer until the client reports feeling peaceful and clear in the event.

Your steadiness is the container. The client's system will only go as deep as it feels the practitioner can hold. The quality of your presence determines the quality of what is possible in the room.

Gathering the Learnings

Once the emotional charge has cleared, ask the unconscious mind and the higher self: what can we learn from this event? What is important to know? What does this experience have to teach?

Receive whatever comes — without evaluation, without steering toward a particular insight, without rushing. Ask again and again: anything else? Keep the space open until the learnings are genuinely complete. Clients will often think they have finished and then, with one more gentle prompt, access the piece that turns out to be most important.

When the learnings feel complete, ask the unconscious mind to preserve them — to hold everything that has been understood and understood deeply, and then to look down at the event from above. Is there anything else visible from this perspective? Any final wisdom before we return?

For sessions involving a younger self in this lifetime, particularly where a child was left in a dangerous or neglectful situation — check whether inner child healing is appropriate. Ask the client: how is your younger self down there? Would you like to go down and connect with them? If yes, guide them gently into the inner child healing, allowing the adult self to bring love, safety, and what was missing in the original moment to the child who needed it. This is some of the most tender and most transformative work in the entire practice. Take your time with it.

> ***Practitioner Note |*** *Inner child healing is not always needed, and the unconscious will indicate when it is. Trust that guidance. When it is needed and done well, when the adult self genuinely meets the child with love rather than performing a technique, the shift it produces is often the most profound of any moment in the session. Clients sometimes cry in a way that is entirely different from grief. They are crying because they are finally receiving something they have been waiting for their whole life.*

Returning to Now

Understanding the Inner Child

The concept of the inner child — that younger part of ourselves still living within our psyche, still carrying unmet needs, unresolved pain, and unfulfilled longings — is one of the most powerful and most tender areas of healing we encounter in RCT practice.

When a child experiences something painful that they do not have the resources to process fully — whether that is overt trauma, chronic neglect, emotional unavailability, shame, abandonment, or simply not having their needs consistently met — that younger self does not simply grow past it. They remain, in a very real sense, waiting. Waiting for the safety, the love, the presence, the acknowledgement that never came. And until that waiting is answered, they continue to influence the adult — through emotional reactivity, through relationship patterns, through the body's responses, through every moment when an old wound gets reactivated by something in the present.

The Inner Child

Every adult carries the children they once were

The child who needed to be seen

The part of you that was overlooked, dismissed, or made to feel invisible. Healing this means finally being witnessed.

The integrated child — carried in the heart

When we heal, we do not leave the child behind. We bring them with us, held in love and wholeness.

The child who needed to be loved

The part of you that longed for warmth, acceptance, and unconditional care. Healing this transforms every relationship.

When we heal the inner child, we heal not just ourselves — but every relationship we carry forward.

The inner child — every adult carries the children they once were, waiting to be met with love and safety.

Some of the clearest signs that inner child healing is needed include: chronic feelings of shame or guilt that feel disproportionate; overworking or constant striving for approval; difficulty being present; patterns of self-sabotage; an inability to celebrate genuine progress; tantrums or emotional flooding that feel younger than the chronological age; and deep difficulties with intimacy, trust, or allowing oneself to be truly seen and loved.

Spiritual Reparenting: What It Actually Is

Reparenting, in the context of RCT, is not a technique. It is an experience. It is the moment when the adult self — or the client's Higher Self, or the compassionate presence of the practitioner holding the space — goes back to meet the child who was left without what they needed, and provides it. Not as a simulation. Not as an exercise. But as a genuine transmission of love, safety, and presence that the nervous system receives as real.

This is what makes inner child work in RCT different from intellectual acknowledgement. We are not asking the client to think about their younger self with compassion. We are facilitating an experience — in the body, in the unconscious, in the Timeline — in which the younger self actually receives what they were waiting for. And when that happens, something resolves that no amount of insight could have touched.

> *Practitioner Note | Inner child work calls for extraordinary gentleness. You are working with the most vulnerable part of a person — the part that learned, in the most formative years of their life, what they could expect from the world and from the people in it. Your presence, your tone, your pace, your care — all of it lands in that younger nervous system. Take your time. Let the client lead. Trust what emerges.*

The Pink Energy Process: Reintegrating the Inner Child

When inner child healing has taken place and the younger self is ready to leave the event and come with the client into the present, RCT uses a specific process of energetic reintegration. This is not purely symbolic — it is an experiential act of wholeness.

Once the adult self has connected with the younger self, offered what was missing, and the child feels ready — guide the client to take a few deep breaths, pumping pink energy of unconditional love from their heart into the child's heart, until a bubble of love forms around the child. With each breath, the child becomes smaller and smaller, held entirely in that loving field, until they are small enough to float gently into the client's heart, where they are held and will always be held.

People sometimes cry at this point. It is important to check the quality of those tears — if they are tears of grief or distress, work with them as you would any emotional release. But often, they are something different entirely: tears of being received. Of a part of the self finally coming home after a very long absence. When that happens, simply hold the space. Let them have it fully.

> *Practitioner Note | When a client re-integrates their inner child in this way, you are witnessing one of the most profound moments in all of healing. Something that has been waiting — sometimes for decades — is finally answered. The adult self becomes, in that moment, the parent the child always needed. Do not rush it. Do not fill the silence. Let the integration complete itself in its own time.*

Inner Child Healing Outside the Session

Part of tending to the inner child is helping clients develop an ongoing, nurturing relationship with their younger selves between sessions. This is not clinical homework — it is the beginning of a different quality of self-relationship. Some clients find it helpful to keep a photo of themselves as a young child and speak to that child with love and reassurance. Others use journalling, meditation, or simply noticing — in a moment of emotional reactivity — that it is a younger part of them that is reacting, and responding with compassion rather than judgment.

Connecting with the inner child also means reconnecting with the natural qualities of childhood that most of us lose under the weight of adult life: wonder, creativity, playfulness, spontaneity, the capacity to be delighted by small things. As the inner child heals and feels genuinely safe, these qualities tend to re-emerge naturally — not as performance, but as an organic return to a more whole and integrated way of being in the world.

And perhaps one of the most beautiful downstream effects: clients who have done deep inner child healing often find that their capacity to be present with the children in their own lives changes profoundly. Having been inside the experience of what a child needs, they find they know how to meet those needs in a way they simply didn't before. The healing moves outward, generation by generation, in exactly the way this whole body of work suggests it will.

Once the learnings are complete and any inner child healing is done, ask the unconscious mind to preserve all the learnings, and then to begin floating back toward the present, only as quickly as it releases the emotion and the limiting belief on every connected event all the way back to now.

Allow time for this. The journey back along the Timeline is not instantaneous, the unconscious is sweeping clean the chain of connected experiences, and that process deserves the space it needs. You may see the client's face shift subtly as they travel, or notice their breathing change. Some clients spontaneously name things they are passing — memories flashing up as the chain resolves. You'll often see their eyes move from side to side as connected memories flash up to resolve. Simply hold the space. They will let you know when they are back above now.

When they return, check what flashed up on the way back? Is it linked to any trauma's or trapped emotional charges mentioned earlier on the Testing Sheet? Then, check whether the unconscious wants to do another round, or whether today's session has reached its natural limit. Trust the answer. Their body knows their capacity best.

If time and the client's energy permit, return to the Testing Sheet and identify the next priority belief from the list. Repeat the process. Up to three beliefs or root cause events per session is generally the natural limit, the unconscious will indicate when it has had enough for today, with responses becoming less clear or the client beginning to show signs of integration fatigue. Respect that limit every time.

Stage 5 Closing the Session

When the healing work for the session is complete, bring the client gently back to full conscious awareness. Ask the unconscious mind to come back down into the body, back into the present moment, back into the room. Eyes closed, they allow everything to integrate. This may take thirty seconds or several minutes. Invite them to take their time. When they are ready, they open their eyes.

Once they are back and grounded, spend time debriefing what arose. Ask them how it was. What came up on the way back from each event? What surprised them? What made sense? What are they sitting with? This conversation is important — not just for the client's integration but for your understanding of what happened and what it means for the sessions ahead. Take notes. The details of what surfaced will inform the pre-filling of the next session's Testing Sheet.

Before the client leaves, ask them to be gentle with themselves in the coming week — in their thoughts, their reactions, their dreams, any shifts in the behaviours or patterns connected to the beliefs that were addressed. Give them a simple framework for noticing the detoxing of emotions that were addressed in the session. Energies that they had been holding onto, for sometimes decades, finally being able to be detoxed. Note, it’s not an assignment to complete, but an invitation to stay curious about what might be changing.

And then. This part matters — acknowledge them. Not effusively, not in a way that feels performative. But with genuine recognition of what they just did. Going to the root of old pain takes real courage. Sitting with what is stored in the body, feeling it fully, releasing it, that is not easy, and it is not nothing. The client who walks out of your room is carrying something lighter than what they walked in with. That deserves to be named.

> ***Practitioner Note |*** *After the client leaves, complete your session notes promptly while everything is fresh. Note the root cause ages that surfaced, the key learnings that emerged, the beliefs that shifted and the ones that still need work, anything that arose that surprised you or that requires particular care in future sessions. We also treat this work like personal development, the client leave sometimes excited and uplifted, wanting to learn more, so we email any relevant resources and positive learnings from the session for the client to continue learning inbetween sessions.*

— — —

When the Session Doesn't Go as Expected

Even with thorough preparation and genuine skill, sessions do not always unfold cleanly. The unconscious may decline to go to a particular event. The client may access something that feels too intense and need to come back out before the release is complete. A belief that tested as ready may lead somewhere unexpected. The emotion may not move as quickly as you anticipated.

None of these are failures. They are the session telling you something. The unconscious that declines is protecting the client — trust it and move to what it will allow. The client who needs to come out of an event needs regulation before they can go back in — bring them up above the Timeline, help them breathe, let the nervous system settle, and then check whether they are ready to continue or whether the session has done enough for today. The unexpected place the belief leads is usually more relevant than where you expected to go — follow it. The emotion that moves slowly needs more time, not more pressure. Hold steady.

The single most important quality in these moments is not technical knowledge. It is presence. The practitioner who stays calm when the session becomes complex gives the client's nervous system permission to stay with what is arising rather than contracting away from it. Your regulated presence is always, in these moments, the most therapeutic thing you can offer.

If you are ever genuinely uncertain what to do — if you are in a session and something has arisen that you do not know how to hold, the answer is almost always the same. Slow down. Return to the breath. Ask the unconscious mind directly what it needs. And trust that thc system you are working with is intelligent, that it knows what it can and cannot process in this moment, and that following its guidance is always safer than overriding it with your own agenda for the session. We can never ask too many questions to their ucm and higher mind, remember, we are the co-pilot their healing.

The Cumulative Program: What Eight to Twelve Sessions Makes Possible

A single RCT session can produce genuine, lasting change. I have seen it happen, and I have felt it happen in my own healing. But the full power of this method is realised across a series of sessions, the cumulative arc of healing that unfolds when root after root is addressed, layer after layer is cleared, and the whole person gradually becomes more themselves.

By sessions four and five, most clients report noticing something has shifted in their daily life, a reaction that did not arise where it always did, a choice they made differently without consciously deciding to, a relationship dynamic that has quietly changed. By sessions eight to twelve, the arc is visible in the Testing Sheet data, the ratings that have moved, the beliefs that now test as true that were deeply embedded when we began, the life domains that have opened.

And there is something else that happens across this arc that the numbers do not quite capture. The client develops a different relationship with themselves. They begin to trust their own body's signals in a way they perhaps never have.

They find that they can meet difficult emotions with curiosity rather than dread, because they have learned — in the most direct possible way, that emotions that are fully felt do not destroy. They complete and release. That knowledge, once it is in the body, changes how a person moves through everything.

That is the gift of the full arc. Not just the healing of specific wounds, but the development of a capacity to continue healing — to recognise when something is being touched, to know what to do with it, to trust the process not just in a session room but in the middle of an ordinary Tuesday when something old and familiar rises up and the person, for the first time, knows how to meet it.

That is what we are building toward, session by session. Not dependency. Capacity. Not a client who needs us indefinitely. A client who has been guided so completely back to themselves that they carry their own healing forward from here.

That is the work. And now you know how to do it.

— — —

Reflection

> *If you were to sit down with an RCT practitioner today, what would you name as the one thing you most want to heal or change — the root beneath the surface?*

Your reflection:

— —

If you would like to become a certified practitioner of RCT, you can find out more and enrol here - https://www.thecentreforhealing.com/root-cause-therapy-certification-1

PART FOUR — SPECIALISED PROTOCOLS

Chapter Thirteen: The Root of Physical Issues

This does not mean that all physical issues are emotional in origin. It does not mean that medical care should be bypassed, or that a person with a serious diagnosis should replace their treatment with healing sessions. It means that the body and the mind are one continuous system, and that when we address the emotional and unconscious dimensions of a physical symptom, when we find and heal the root that the symptom may be expressing — we sometimes see things resolve that nothing else has been able to touch.

I have seen this. Chronic pain that cleared when its emotional root was addressed. Autoimmune symptoms that settled as the nervous system regulation improved through healing work. Fatigue that lifted when suppressed grief was finally allowed to move. Digestive issues that resolved when the anxiety driving them was healed at the source. I am not making claims about causation in every case. I am reporting what I have observed — consistently, across many years and many clients, when we treat the whole person rather than the symptom alone.

This chapter gives you the framework and the protocol for working with physical issues in RCT. It is one of the most profound areas of this practice, and one that requires particular care, particular humility, and a genuine commitment to holding the medical and the emotional in respectful relationship with each other.

Why the Body Speaks What the Mind Cannot

The brain runs the body. This is not a metaphor — it is physiology. Every organ, every system, every cellular process in the body is regulated by the brain and nervous system, which means that everything happening in the emotional and unconscious mind has a direct line of influence to physical function. When the emotional system is under sustained stress, when unprocessed emotions are locked in the body, when the nervous system is chronically activated, when the unconscious is holding beliefs and experiences that keep the system in a state of low-grade emergency, the physical body reflects that state. Not immediately, and not always obviously. But over time, consistently, and often in ways that carry the fingerprint of the emotional experience that generated them.

In Root-Cause Therapy, we understand physical issues as potentially having several emotional and unconscious dimensions, and we hold all of them in awareness when working with a client who presents with physical symptoms.

The first is suppressed emotion. Emotions that are not expressed and processed do not disappear — they are stored in the body. When they accumulate over time without resolution, the unconscious mind eventually begins to express them through physical channels. Pain, illness, and chronic conditions can be the body's last resort, the loudest available signal that something unprocessed is demanding attention. The specific location and nature of the symptom sometimes carries meaning in relation to the emotion that is stored there, though we approach this with curiosity rather than assumption.

The second is what we call the unconscious payoff. This is perhaps the most delicate concept in this chapter, and it needs to be introduced to clients with exceptional care and without any suggestion of blame. The premise is this: the unconscious mind is always trying to meet fundamental human needs. If a person grew up in an environment where emotional attention and care were only available when they were sick, where illness was the one reliable way to receive love, rest, or connection, the unconscious may have formed a deep association between physical symptoms and having those needs met. This is not a conscious or deliberate choice. It is an unconscious programme, running below awareness, that keeps recreating the physical condition because the emotional payoff — care, attention, permission to rest — still feels essential and still feels unavailable in any other form.

The third is chronic stress and nervous system dysregulation. The stress response, the activation of the adrenal system in response to perceived threat — is designed to be temporary. It is designed to mobilise the body for survival in a moment of danger, and then to resolve when the danger passes. When a person lives in chronic stress, whether from external circumstances, from relentless self-pressure, from patterns of people-pleasing or martyrdom or perpetual overgiving, the adrenal system never gets to fully reset. The body's resources for healing and immune function are perpetually diverted to managing the stress response. And over time, the system begins to break down in the areas of greatest vulnerability.

The fourth is genealogical patterning — physical conditions, health tendencies, and body-based beliefs that have been passed down through family lines, sometimes for many generations. We will explore this in more depth in the next chapter on generational trauma. For now, it is enough to note that when a client presents with a physical condition that runs in their family, the genealogical dimension is always worth exploring in the healing work.

The body is not lying. It is not malfunctioning without reason. It is communicating — through the only language that has not yet been silenced, that something underneath needs to be heard.

The Protocol for Working With Physical Issues

The following protocol is the structured approach we use in RCT when a client's primary presenting concern is a physical issue or chronic condition. It adapts the standard session framework to ensure that the physical dimension is fully integrated into the healing work from the very first session.

1. Intake form review. Before the first session, read the client's intake form carefully with the physical symptoms held in primary focus. Note when the symptoms began, what was happening in the client's life at that time, whether there is a family history of similar conditions, and any relevant medical context. Pre-fill the Testing Sheet accordingly, including the physical section at the top right of the sheet.

2. First session: intake conversation. Begin by reviewing the intake form with the client directly — going over their history, clarifying the timeline of the physical symptoms, and establishing the overarching goal for the healing work. Be clear with the client from the outset: you cannot guarantee that physical issues will resolve through this work, but you will do everything in your power to address every emotional and unconscious root that may be contributing. Honesty about this establishes trust and sets realistic expectations.

3. Intention setting. In the Intention field of the Testing Sheet, help the client articulate a milestone goal that moves toward physical relief. This should be specific and felt rather than abstract — not 'I want to be healthy' but something like 'I want to wake up without pain in my lower back' or 'I want to have enough energy to be present with my children.' A felt intention creates a more direct line to the unconscious than a conceptual one.

4. Emotions review. As you go through the emotions section of the Testing Sheet, ask specifically whether something significant was happening emotionally when the physical

symptoms first began — or in the period leading up to them. A grief, a loss, a significant stressor, a relationship breakdown, a period of sustained overwork or self-neglect. The answer will not always be immediately available to the conscious mind, but asking the question opens the door and gives the unconscious permission to bring the connection forward.

5. Client feedback ratings. As you work through the life domain ratings, pay particular attention to the areas that are scoring very high in stress or very low in peace, energy, and physical health. These give you a picture of where the system is most taxed and where the healing work may have the most systemic impact.

6. Physical monitoring. Note in the physical section of the Testing Sheet the specific symptoms, their severity on a scale of one to ten, their location, and their quality — sharp, dull, constant, intermittent. Track these ratings session to session. Physical symptoms do not always shift immediately after healing sessions — sometimes there is a lag as the system integrates — but the trend across sessions will tell you whether the work is reaching the root.

7. Limiting beliefs — body beliefs specifically. After working through the core limiting beliefs on the Level 1 Testing Sheet, take the client through the body-related beliefs on the Extended Testing Sheet. Beliefs such as I am ashamed of my body, I love my body, it is safe for me to be healthy, it serves me to have an illness, being sick allows me to feel loved or cared for. These body-specific beliefs often surface the

unconscious payoff dimension and can point directly toward the emotional root of physical symptoms.

8. Past healing — targeting the physical. Once ready for the regression, pre-mark the beliefs, emotions, and events that are most likely to be connected to the physical symptoms. And when you open the Timeline and ask for the root cause, you can ask the unconscious mind directly: what is the root cause of this physical condition, the first event, which, when healed, will allow the body to return to health? Trust what arises, even if it is not what the conscious mind expected.

9. Future healing for illness anxiety. If the client is carrying significant anxiety about their physical condition — fear of diagnosis, catastrophic thinking about what the symptoms might mean, hypervigilance around their body — consider a future healing session once the initial past work has been done. Take them to a future where they experience themselves as fully healthy and vibrant. Allow them to feel that state completely, receive the wisdom and advice of their future self, and integrate that energy into their cells before returning to the present. The affirmations that naturally arise from their future self's advice can be sent to them as reminders between sessions.

> ***Practitioner Note |*** *Always encourage clients with physical conditions to continue with their medical care alongside the healing work. RCT is not a replacement for medical treatment — it is a complement to it. Frame it clearly: we are addressing the emotional and*

> *unconscious dimensions that may be contributing to what your body is experiencing. Everything else your medical team is doing continues alongside this. This framing is both clinically responsible and practically important for the therapeutic relationship.*

— — —

When the Root Is Found

I want to share a composite of what this work can look like, drawn from my years of experience with clients presenting with physical symptoms, because the theory becomes most real through the specific.

A client came to me — I will call her A — after years of on-and-off burnout. She was extraordinarily capable, always the person others relied on, but she could not switch off. Her nervous system was perpetually activated, and her body had begun to reflect it — chronic fatigue, persistent tension in her neck and shoulders that no amount of massage or physiotherapy had been able to address, and a pattern of falling ill every time she took a holiday, as though her body was waiting for a moment of stillness to finally collapse.

When we looked at the intake form, something stood out. She described herself as someone who had never felt she could stop — not even as a child. When we explored this in the first session, she described growing up with a parent whose emotional wellbeing had been fragile and unpredictable. As a child, she had learned — not through any explicit instruction but through the pattern of experience, that if she was vigilant, if she stayed useful, if she never stopped and never needed anything, things at home felt safer. The chronic activation in her body was not a medical mystery. It was a faithful expression of a nervous system that had been running a survival programme since childhood and had never received the signal that it was finally safe to rest.

We worked with the root of that pattern across several sessions. The belief that she was only safe if she was useful. The grief of the child who had never been allowed to simply be. The moment, early in her life, where the unconscious had formed the conclusion that stopping meant danger.

After those sessions, her neck tension reduced significantly. The pattern of collapse-on-holiday resolved. Her energy, the real, sustainable kind, not the adrenaline-driven variety she had been running on — began to return. Her body had not been malfunctioning. It had been trying, in the only way available to it, to communicate something that had been waiting decades to be heard.

That is what this protocol makes possible. Not a guarantee. Not a replacement for medical care. But a genuine, often profound complement to it, the work that addresses the human being inside the physical condition, and trusts that when the root is healed, the body knows how to find its way back toward health.

The next chapter turns to one of the most important, and most frequently overlooked — sources of physical and emotional patterning: what we inherit. Not just genetically, but in the deepest layers of our nervous system, our beliefs, and our unconscious responses to the world. Generational and natal trauma. The wounds that arrive before we have even drawn our first breath.

———

Reflection

> *Is there anywhere in your life where you sense that a physical symptom or pattern in your body might be connected to something emotional, unresolved, or inherited rather than purely physical?*

Your reflection:

Chapter Fourteen: Generational and Natal Trauma

The patterns are real. The wounds are real. They simply did not originate where we assumed they did.

The Science: How Trauma Travels Through Generations

In 2013, a research team at Emory University published findings from a study that stopped the scientific community in its tracks — not because it was speculative, but because it was precise, replicable, and impossible to dismiss.

The researchers exposed adult male mice to the scent of cherry blossoms while simultaneously administering a mild electric shock. The mice quickly developed a conditioned fear response, the scent of cherry blossoms became associated with threat, and their nervous systems responded accordingly. So far, unremarkable. Conditioned fear responses in mice had been studied for decades.

What was remarkable was what happened next. The offspring of these mice, who had never been exposed to the scent of cherry blossoms, who had never experienced any shock, who had been raised in an entirely separate environment — showed the same fear response to the smell. Their nervous systems reacted to cherry blossoms as though they themselves had experienced the trauma that their fathers had experienced. The grandchildren of the original mice showed it too.

The mechanism was epigenetic. The traumatic experience had not altered[8] the mice's DNA sequence — their genes were unchanged. What changed was the expression of those genes. The fear response had been encoded at an epigenetic level and transmitted to subsequent generations through the germline, meaning that the biological inheritance of trauma is not metaphor. It is measurable. It is specific. And it passes through us to our children and our children's children until something intervenes to break the chain.

The implications for human beings are profound, and for practitioners working with trauma, they are transformative. Because it means that what a client carries is not only the product of their own experiences. It is the accumulated, encoded residue of what their parents, grandparents, and ancestors experienced — their wars, their famines, their losses, their violations, their fears. All of it potentially present in the nervous system of the person sitting across from you, shaping their responses to the world, making them afraid of things they have no conscious reason to fear, limiting them in ways that their personal history alone cannot explain.

We do not only inherit our ancestors' eyes and their cheekbones. We inherit their unresolved fears, their unfelt grief, their interrupted survival responses. Until those are healed, they travel forward through time in the bodies of their descendants.

What Genealogical Trauma Looks Like in Sessions

When the unconscious mind indicates that the root cause of a presenting pattern is genealogical, when the answer to "was it before, during, or after your birth?" is "before, in a previous generation" — what the client accesses in the regression is not their own memory. It is the memory held in the family line. The experience of a parent, a grandparent, a great-grandparent, sometimes several generations back.

This can be disorienting for clients the first time it happens, and it requires careful, steady holding from the practitioner. The client may find themselves in a body that is not theirs, in a time and place they have no conscious knowledge of, experiencing emotions and circumstances that belong to an ancestor. And yet the emotional charge is as real and as present as anything from their own personal history because at the level of the nervous system, it is present. It has been carried forward in the body's cellular memory, and it is as alive as the day it was first created.

The most important thing to understand about genealogical healing is that its effects extend in both directions through time. When we heal a generational wound in the healing session, when the emotional charge is released and the limiting beliefs formed by that ancestral experience are cleared, the healing does not just affect the present client. It ripples backward through the lineage, completing something that was left incomplete perhaps generations ago. And it ripples forward, breaking the chain so that what would otherwise have continued to be transmitted to the client's children and grandchildren is stopped here, in this session, in this body, in this lifetime.

That is extraordinary work. And it is available in every session, whenever the unconscious indicates it is needed.

My Own Generational Trauma: Food Scarcity

I want to share something personal here, because I think it illustrates more clearly than any clinical description what it feels like to discover that a pattern you have struggled with your entire life did not actually originate with you.

For as long as I can remember, I had an unusual and uncomfortable relationship with food — specifically with the fear that there would not be enough. It was not connected to anything obvious in my own childhood. My family was not wealthy, but we were not without food. The anxiety around scarcity was disproportionate to any experience I could consciously recall, and it had a quality that felt almost pre-verbal — as though it had been present before I had language for it.

When I eventually explored this in my own healing work, what the unconscious surfaced was not from my personal history. It was genealogical. What came through was the lived experience of an ancestor who had known genuine food scarcity — not as a temporary difficulty, but as a sustained, survival-level deprivation that had imprinted deeply on the nervous system and been encoded in the family line. My anxiety was not irrational. It was the faithful transmission of a real fear that had belonged, originally, to someone who had every reason to feel it.

When that was healed, when the ancestral emotional charge was released and the unconscious understood that the scarcity was not happening now, had not been my experience, and did not need to continue being transmitted — something shifted that years of conscious work around food had not been able to touch. The anxiety around food did not just reduce. It resolved. Because the root had finally been found and healed, not in my own history, but in the history that had been living in my body through inheritance.

This is what genealogical healing makes possible. Not just understanding where a pattern came from. Healing it at the source, and freeing everyone who comes after from having to carry it.

— — —

Natal Trauma: What Happens Before We Are Born

The second dimension of this chapter is natal trauma, the experiences and imprints that occur in the womb, during birth, and in the earliest weeks and months of life, before the conscious mind has developed the capacity to process or even to record experience in any conventional sense.

The idea that pre-birth experience shapes us is not new. It is supported by decades of research in pre- and perinatal psychology, pioneered by figures such as Dr. David Chamberlain and Dr. Thomas Verny[10,11], who demonstrated that the developing infant in the womb is not a passive biological entity but a sensitive, responsive being whose nervous system is already forming responses to the emotional environment of the mother, the quality of the relationship between the parents, the stress or peace of the household, and significant events in the outer world.

What the mother feels, the foetus registers. Not with the cognitive complexity of an adult, but with the somatic sensitivity of a nervous system that is entirely undefended and entirely attuned to its environment. A mother who is deeply anxious throughout a pregnancy transmits a neurochemical environment of stress to the developing child. A mother who is grieving, or frightened, or in a relationship that does not feel safe, the child in the womb registers this, and the nervous system forms its first responses to the world accordingly.

These responses are not conscious beliefs. They are preverbal, somatic, and often extraordinarily difficult to access through conventional therapeutic approaches because they were formed before language, before narrative, before any capacity to make meaning of experience. They live in the deepest layer of the nervous system, shaping the most fundamental sense of whether the world is safe, whether one is wanted, whether existence itself is welcome.

In RCT sessions, natal trauma can surface when the unconscious indicates the root cause of a pattern lies before birth — during gestation or during the birth process itself. What the client accesses in these regressions is not visual memory in any conventional sense. It may be felt as sensation, as darkness or light, as a quality of emotional tone rather than a scene or a story. The practitioner's role in these moments is to follow with particular gentleness — asking not what they see but what they feel, what they sense, what is present in the body, and to trust that whatever arises is exactly what needs to be addressed.

> ***Practitioner Note |*** *When working with natal or pre-birth material, shift your language entirely to sensation and feeling. "What do you notice in your body?" rather than "What do you see?" "What is the quality of this place?" rather than "Can you describe what is around you?" The foetal experience is somatic and sensory rather than visual or narrative, and visual language can inadvertently create pressure that blocks access. Meet the client in the body, and the body will show you what is there.*

Relationship Patterns That Begin Before Birth

Some of the most powerful and unexpected genealogical and natal work I have witnessed in sessions has been with clients whose most significant relationship patterns — their attachment style, their fundamental sense of whether love is safe, their deepest beliefs about whether they are wanted and welcomed — traced back not to childhood experiences but to what they absorbed in the womb about the relationship between their parents.

A child developing in a womb where the parents' relationship is volatile, or cold, or where one parent is absent or rejecting, absorbs that relational template as their first experience of what love and connection look and feel like. Not through any conscious learning, but through the neurochemical environment — through the cocktail of stress hormones or oxytocin or cortisol that the mother's emotional state produces and that the developing nervous system bathes in for months.

Clients who access this material in sessions sometimes discover that the relationship pattern they have been struggling with their entire adult life, the inability to trust, the expectation of abandonment, the sense that love is always conditional or always about to be withdrawn — has its deepest root not in anything that happened to them personally, but in what they witnessed and absorbed before they were born. And when that root is healed, when the nervous system finally receives a different message at the level where the original imprint was formed, the shift can be among the most profound and the most lasting that this work produces.

Practitioner Spotlight

Fabienne — RCT Certified Practitioner

The following case demonstrates something that surprises many practitioners when they first encounter it: the reach of generational and natal trauma extends not only across human generations, but into the animals who share our lives and our emotional fields. Fabienne, a certified RCT practitioner, shares what happened when she worked with a client whose dog was displaying symptoms that no conventional explanation had been able to account for.

My client Hanna came to me not for herself initially, but for her dog Finn. Finn had developed severe anxiety — trembling, inability to settle, fearfulness in situations that had never previously bothered him. The vet had found nothing physically wrong. Hanna was at a loss.

In our sessions, we began working with Hanna herself — her own anxiety, her own history, the patterns in her family line. What emerged was a significant thread of inherited fear and instability running through several generations. As we worked with this material and began to release it, something unexpected happened. Finn's anxiety began to settle. Session by session, as Hanna's own nervous system regulation improved and the generational charge began to clear, Finn became calmer. More settled. More himself.

What I witnessed in this work confirmed something I had begun to suspect: that the animals in our lives are not separate from our emotional field. They absorb what we carry. And when we heal what we carry, they can release what they have been holding in response to it. Hanna did not come to heal herself. But in healing herself — in healing what had been passed down to her — she healed Finn too.

— Fabienne Wylder, RCT Certified Practitioner
https://www.fabiennewydler.com/

This story illustrates something that the science of epigenetics and the evidence from thousands of RCT sessions continues to confirm: the reach of unhealed trauma, and the reach of healing, extends further than we have been taught to imagine. It moves through family lines. It lives in the bodies of the people, and sometimes the animals, who inhabit our closest emotional world. And when we heal it at the root, the effect does not stay contained to the individual in the session room. It ripples.

— — —

Holding the Bigger Picture as a Practitioner

Working with generational and natal material requires a particular quality of openness from the practitioner, a willingness to hold a much larger frame of time and causation than most conventional training has prepared us for. When a client accesses a memory that is not theirs, or drops into pre-birth experience that feels entirely unlike the visual narratives of later childhood memories, the practitioner who has not made peace with this territory can inadvertently communicate doubt or discomfort that causes the client to close down.

Your job in these moments is not to evaluate the philosophical or scientific status of what is arising. Your job is to hold steady, to follow the client's experience with genuine curiosity and complete acceptance, and to apply the same healing process — release the emotion, gather the learnings, clear the charge, return to now — regardless of where in time or across how many generations the root cause has been located.

The unconscious mind is not confused about this. It knows exactly where the root is. It surfaces what it surfaces because it is ready to be healed. Trust that intelligence. And bring to it the same quality of presence and care that you would bring to any other material because for the nervous system, there is no difference. The pain is equally real. The release is equally complete. And the freedom on the other side is equally available, regardless of whether the wound was formed in this lifetime or in the one that came before.

In the next chapter, we turn to the healing of relationships — one of the richest and most transformative areas of this work, and the one where the generational and natal roots we have explored in this chapter most visibly and most consequentially express themselves in present-day life.

Practitioner Spotlight

Alena Turley — RCT Certified Practitioner

Alena Turley is an RCT certified practitioner who worked with Erica over four Root Cause Therapy sessions and ongoing somatic support. Erica came to Alena carrying a weight that had accumulated across decades and generations — overwhelming grief following the sudden death of her mother, chronic fatigue, a marriage strained by disconnection, and a deep sense of not feeling heard. What unfolded through their work together illustrates how intergenerational patterns, when finally seen and released, can shift the ground beneath everything.

Erica arrived at our first session feeling depleted and overwhelmed. She was managing her daughter Bella's mental health challenges, carrying unprocessed grief for her mother, dealing with adrenal fatigue, and struggling to feel safe or connected in her marriage. She and her husband had different love languages, and the gap between them had grown into a distance she didn't know how to cross.

The testing revealed a cluster of limiting beliefs — "I am heard," "I know my purpose," "safe to relax," "I fear success," "I fear conflict," "life is hard" — all testing as not true in her unconscious. When we followed these roots, what emerged was not primarily Erica's own story. It was her mother's, and her grandmother's before that.

The belief "safe to relax" traced all the way back to birth — the intergenerational expectation placed on the eldest daughter to perform, transmitted from mother to daughter without conscious awareness across generations. The belief "I fear conflict" traced two generations back to her grandmother, who had turned a blind eye to her husband's behaviour because submission was all she had been permitted to know. Erica had been carrying these patterns as though they were her own, living inside a story that had been written long before she arrived.

What struck me most was the speed at which these realisations translated into her daily life. By our second session, just three weeks after the first, Erica reported that she had "turned a corner" in her marriage. She was feeling heard. She was setting boundaries. There was more intimacy, more ease. She had not done this by working on her marriage directly — she had done it by healing what lay beneath her patterns. When the roots shifted, the relationship shifted too.

A particularly significant moment came in our third session, when we traced her fear of conflict to her grandmother's era. As Erica sat with the image of her grandmother — a woman who had no choice but to be silent — she said something I have not forgotten: "It's a new era. We are working it out as we go along. We need to give ourselves so much compassion as we work it out." That was not a reframe I had offered her. It arose from within her own healing. She had found the perspective that set her free.

The work also brought an unexpected gift to her parenting. Understanding that these patterns had been transmitted generationally — not through malice, but through unconscious repetition — gave her the compassion to parent her own daughters differently. By the time we completed our RCT sessions, Bella had settled into high school with far greater ease than anyone had anticipated.

— Alena Turley, RCT Certified Practitioner
https://www.alenaturley.com/

That phrase — "self-worth is intrinsic, not something you build" — is one that arose naturally in Erica's second session and stayed with her. It encapsulates something essential about generational healing: the patterns we have inherited often share a common root in the belief that worth must be earned, that love is conditional, that safety depends on performance. When we trace these beliefs back to where they formed — and back further, to the generations in which they first took hold — we do not just free the individual in front of us. We free the line. The grandmother who had no choice becomes the ancestor whose sacrifice is finally honoured. And the granddaughter carries something forward into her own daughters that was never available to the women who came before.

— — —

In the next chapter, we turn to the healing of relationships — one of the richest and most transformative areas of this work, and the one where the generational and natal roots we have explored in this chapter most visibly and most consequentially express themselves in present-day life.

— — —

Reflection

> *Are there patterns, fears, or tendencies in your life that feel like they didn't quite come from your own direct experience — that feel older, or borrowed? What might they be carrying from the generations before you?*

Your reflection:

— — —

Chapter Fifteen: Healing Relationships

And those lessons, encoded in the nervous system long before we had the cognitive capacity to evaluate them — run forward into every subsequent relationship, shaping who we choose, how we behave, what we trigger in others, and what we allow ourselves to receive. Until they are healed at the root, they do not change. The names change. The faces change. The circumstances change. But the pattern persists, with a fidelity that can feel, from the inside, like destiny.

It is not destiny. It is an unhealed wound expressing itself through the only channels available to it. And it can be healed.

The Self-Fulfilling Prophecy of Relationship Wounds

One of the most important things to understand about relationship patterns is how they perpetuate themselves — not through bad luck or a shortage of good partners, but through the unconscious logic of the nervous system seeking confirmation of what it already believes.

Imagine a child who, early in life, experiences the loss of a parent's presence — not necessarily through death or abandonment, but through emotional unavailability, inconsistency, or the disruption of a relationship that felt central to their safety. The nervous system draws a conclusion: people leave. And that conclusion, once encoded, begins to operate as a perceptual filter. The child, growing into an adult, will notice the evidence that confirms this belief, the small withdrawal, the moment of distance, the partner who is less present on a difficult day, and unconsciously discount or simply not register the evidence that contradicts it. The warmth. The consistency. The love that has been reliably present for years.

More than this, and this is the part that is most difficult to hear, and most important to understand, the nervous system will often unconsciously recreate the conditions that confirm its belief. The person who fears abandonment may push people away when they feel too close, creating the very distance they most dread. They may choose partners who are emotionally unavailable, because availability feels unfamiliar and therefore threatening. They may interpret neutral behaviour as withdrawal, and respond with a reaction that genuinely does cause their partner to pull back. The self-fulfilling prophecy is not malice and it is not stupidity. It is the nervous system doing exactly what nervous systems do — seeking to confirm the map of the world it built in childhood, because a confirmed map, however painful, feels safer than an uncertain one.

Understanding this is essential for practitioners working with relationship patterns, because it reframes what clients are doing in their relationships in a way that is compassionate rather than pathologising. They are not broken. They are not choosing badly. They are faithfully re-enacting the template they were given, and the work is to find that template, heal it at the source, and allow a new one to form in its place.

We do not keep choosing the wrong people. We keep choosing from the same wounded map, until the map is healed. When the root changes, what we are able to see, and to receive — changes with it.

Where Relationship Patterns Begin: Earlier Than You Think

As we explored in the previous chapter, the nervous system's first template for relationship is formed before birth. The developing infant in the womb is immersed in the emotional environment of the mother — her stress hormones, her oxytocin, her grief or her joy, the quality of her relationship with the father, the felt sense of whether this new life is welcomed or complicated or feared.

These pre-birth impressions form the deepest layer of the relational template. They are the most preverbal, the most somatic, and the most difficult to access through conventional approaches — but in RCT, when the unconscious indicates that the root of a relationship pattern lies in the womb, we can go there. We follow the sensations rather than the images, the quality of feeling rather than the narrative, and we apply the same healing process — release, learn, return, that we apply to any other root cause event.

What clients sometimes discover in this work is that their fundamental sense of whether they are wanted, the bedrock question beneath every relationship pattern was formed before they had their first breath. A mother who was ambivalent about the pregnancy, or frightened, or unsupported, or in a relationship that was already breaking, the child in that womb absorbs the emotional quality of that context and forms their first, deepest conclusion about whether their existence is welcome. Healing that imprint does not erase what happened. But it updates the nervous system's response to it. And that update, at the deepest layer of the relational template, can shift patterns that decades of conscious relationship work could not move.

> ***Practitioner Note |*** *When exploring womb-level relationship material, ask the client to notice the felt quality of the space they are in — is it warm or cold? Expansive or contracted? Welcoming or braced? These somatic qualities often carry the most precise information about the emotional environment the developing child was absorbing. Trust what the client reports and follow it into the release and the learnings with the same thoroughness you would bring to any other event.*

The Push-Pull Pattern: When Closeness Feels Like Danger

One of the most common relationship patterns I have worked with across thousands of sessions is what I think of as the push-pull, the person who desperately wants closeness and connection, but who, when they get it, finds themselves flooded with anxiety and begins unconsciously to create distance. The cycle is exhausting for both parties. The person experiencing it often cannot explain it, even to themselves. They want the relationship. They also cannot bear to be fully in it. And the partner, receiving alternating warmth and withdrawal, typically responds in ways that confirm the original fear — eventually pulling back, becoming guarded, or leaving altogether.

I worked with a client — I will call him M, who came to me with exactly this pattern. He was in his late thirties, articulate about his difficulties, and had done a significant amount of therapeutic work over many years. He understood, at the conscious level, that he had an anxious attachment style. He could explain it fluently. But understanding it had not changed it.

In our first RCT session, we tested the belief: it is safe to be loved. The body swayed backward immediately and clearly. When we asked the unconscious mind for the root cause of this, what arose was not a relationship from his adult life, nor even from his teenage years. It was a moment from very early childhood, a specific night when he had been frightened and called out, and no one had come. Not because his parents were negligent or uncaring — they were, by his own account, essentially good people. But that night, in that moment, the nervous system of a very young child had formed a conclusion: when I am at my most vulnerable, I will be alone.

That single, specific, unremarkable night — unremarkable to everyone except the nervous system that recorded it — had been running his relationship life for three decades. The anxiety when people got close was the nervous system bracing for the moment when they would inevitably not be there. The pushing away was a pre-emptive strike — ending the connection before the inevitable abandonment could occur.

We went to that event on the Timeline. We released what the small child had felt, the fear, the loneliness, the hurt of calling out and not being answered. We gathered the learnings. We did inner child healing, bringing his adult self back to that night to sit with the child who had waited alone, to give him what had been missing. And when he returned along the Timeline to the present, the charge on the belief had gone. When we tested it again — it is safe to be loved, the body swayed forward.

In the weeks that followed, he reported something he had not been able to access before: the capacity to stay present when his partner moved toward him. The anxiety did not arise in the same way. The urge to create distance did not have the same grip. The root had been addressed, and the pattern — without the root to sustain it — had lost its power.

Working With Relationship Beliefs

The Extended Testing Sheet contains a dedicated section of relationship-specific beliefs that are invaluable when working with clients whose primary presenting concerns are relational. These beliefs cover the most common and most consequential relationship patterns, and testing through them at the start of a relationship-focused session gives the practitioner an immediate map of which unconscious conclusions are most active and most ready to be addressed.

The beliefs include: relationships lead to pain, love is meant to feel stressful or unsafe, I fear deep connection, I am better off alone, I always get abandoned, I always get betrayed, I fear commitment, I fear deep connection, it is safe for me to be loved, jealousy and control is love, physical intimacy is shameful, I am worthless, and love is meant to be painful. Each of these, when it tests as not true in the unconscious, points toward a specific relational wound with a specific root, and the regression that follows the testing will find that root with a precision that conscious exploration rarely achieves.

The relationship beliefs often connect directly to the generational and natal material we explored in the previous chapter. A client whose parents modelled a relationship characterised by volatility or control may carry the belief that love is meant to feel unsafe — not because they consciously endorse that view, but because the nervous system formed its template for love inside that environment and has been running that template ever since. When we find the root and heal it, the belief updates, and with it, the nervous system's sense of what love is supposed to feel like.

> ***Practitioner Note |*** *Relationship work often surfaces strong emotion very quickly, particularly grief, the grief of not having been loved in the way the person needed, the grief of relationships lost or damaged by patterns the client now understands but could not previously see. Create space for this grief to move. It is not a detour from the work. It is the work. The healing of relationship wounds is often primarily the healing of grief — for what was not received, for what was taken, for what was unknowingly given away in the hope of finally feeling loved.*

When the System Shuts Down: Working With Dissociation

One specific pattern that arises in relationship healing work, and that requires particular care and particular skill — is dissociation. Dissociation is the nervous system's response to overwhelm that goes beyond what fight or flight can manage. When a threat is too large, too inescapable, or too prolonged for the active survival responses to address, the system can disconnect — producing a state of emotional numbness, unreality, detachment from the body, or the sense of watching oneself from a distance.

In the context of relationship trauma, dissociation often develops as a protective response to abuse, violation, or sustained emotional danger within close relationships, particularly in childhood, when escape was not possible and the threat was coming from the very person on whom survival depended. The disconnection that protected the child in those moments can become a chronic pattern in adulthood, a default response to emotional intensity, to conflict, to intimacy itself, that cuts the person off from their own experience precisely when connection is most available and most needed.

I worked with a client who had developed exactly this pattern. I will call her N. She had experienced significant relational trauma in childhood, and as an adult she found that in moments of emotional closeness or conflict with her partner, she would simply disappear internally. Not dramatically — there was no outward sign. But inside, she was gone. Watching from somewhere behind her own eyes, unable to feel, unable to respond authentically, waiting for the moment to pass so she could return.

Working with dissociation in RCT requires adjusting the approach. Moving too quickly into the root cause event with a client who dissociates easily can trigger the very disconnection we are trying to heal. Instead, we work slowly and relationally — building the therapeutic relationship first, ensuring the client feels genuinely safe in the room, using grounding and somatic anchoring before any Timeline work begins. We check with the unconscious whether it is ready to approach the material, and we respect every "no" without question. And we work with the dissociation itself as a presenting pattern — finding its root, understanding what it was protecting against, and gently, over multiple sessions, creating the conditions in which the nervous system learns that it is finally safe to stay present.

When that happens, when a client who has spent years behind glass finally feels themselves arrive in their own experience, the shift is among the most moving things I have witnessed in this work. Not dramatic. Quiet. The difference between watching your own life from a distance and actually being in it.

> ***Practitioner Note |*** *If a client begins to dissociate during a session — signs include a glassy or distant look, slowed or absent verbal responses, a sudden flatness in the face or voice — bring them back gently before continuing. Ask them to feel their feet on the floor. Ask them to name five things they can see in the room. Breathe with them. Ask them to bring in a memory or imagined place or person that makes them feel safe. Do not push into the material while they are disconnected, the healing cannot reach where the client is not present. Safety and groundedness always come first.*

— — —

Practitioner Spotlight

Jenny Carver — RCT Certified Practitioner

Jenny Carver is a certified RCT practitioner whose own healing journey, and the transformation of her client Natalie — illustrates what becomes possible when relationship wounds are addressed at their root. Natalie came to Jenny carrying patterns that had followed her through every significant relationship in her adult life. What follows is drawn from Jenny's account of that work.

Natalie had been in and out of relationships her whole adult life that followed the same arc — intense connection at the beginning, a gradual sense of suffocation as the other person got closer, and then a pulling away that she could not stop even when she wanted to. She described it as watching herself destroy something she wanted to keep, unable to intervene.

In our sessions, we worked through the relationship beliefs on the Testing Sheet — almost every one of them tested as not true in the unconscious. Love is unsafe. I am always abandoned. I fear deep connection. I am better off alone. We went to the roots, one by one, across several sessions. What we found was a consistent theme: closeness had never felt safe. The relationships she had observed and experienced early in her life had taught her nervous system that the people who were supposed to be closest were also the most unpredictable, the most likely to hurt.

By the time we had addressed the core roots, something had shifted that Natalie described as structural — not just a change in how she felt, but in how she perceived. She started noticing her partner's consistency in a way she never had before. She could let him close without the familiar wave of panic. She told me in our final session: "I feel like I can finally stay."

— Jenny Carver, RCT Certified Practitioner
www.jennycarver.com

I feel like I can finally stay. That sentence carries everything. Not just the shift in a relationship, but the shift in a person's entire experience of connection, the difference between a nervous system braced for inevitable loss and one that has finally received the signal that it is safe to arrive.

— — —

Relationship healing is rarely the work of a single session, or even a short series. The patterns are layered, the roots are often multiple, and the nervous system's recalibration toward safety in connection takes time and consistent reinforcement. But the direction of travel, once the root work has begun, is unmistakable. And the relationships that become possible on the other side of that healing, the quality of connection, the genuine intimacy, the capacity to both give and receive love without the wound distorting everything — are among the most compelling demonstrations of what this work is ultimately for.

In the next chapter, we turn to two of the most complex and most common presentations in healing practice: mental health and addiction. These are the areas where the conventional system has often failed people most profoundly, and where root-cause work has the most to offer.

— — —

Reflection

> *Do you notice a recurring pattern in your close relationships — a shape that seems to repeat regardless of the person? If that pattern could speak, what would it say it's protecting you from?*

Your reflection:

— — —

Chapter Sixteen: Mental Health — Anxiety, Depression and Grief

This chapter is about how we do that — with three of the most common and most consequential presentations you will encounter in practice. Anxiety. Depression. Grief. Each one has its own character, its own root-cause landscape, its own clinical considerations. And each one, when approached through the RCT framework, opens in ways that the conventional system has rarely been able to reach.

Anxiety: The Past Projected Into the Future

Anxiety is one of the most precise and most elegant examples of what happens when an emotion is interrupted and not allowed to complete. At its root, anxiety is almost always fear — fear that was experienced at a moment in the past when there was no safe adult present, no language for what was happening, no capacity to express or process what the nervous system was registering. The fear response was activated. It was not completed. And the incomplete loop, the survival signal that never received an all-clear — is stored in the body, where it continues to run.

What makes anxiety feel so urgent, so present, so inescapable is this: the body does not know time. What is stored from the past is experienced as now. The fear of the five-year-old who was unsafe, who had no one to turn to, who lay awake listening to something frightening in the next room, that fear, unprocessed, lives in the adult body as though it is still happening. And the unconscious mind, seeking to protect the person from being surprised by danger again, projects that stored fear forward as worst-case scenarios — future images, catastrophic predictions, the relentless anticipation of things going wrong.

This is why anxiety is so resistant to reassurance. Telling an anxious person that everything will be fine does not reach the place where the fear is stored. The nervous system is not receiving reassurance — it is receiving more words that it cannot integrate, because the root of the activation is not a thought that can be argued with. It is an experience that needs to be completed.

Understanding this — really understanding it — changes how we sit with anxious clients. We are not there to calm them down or talk them out of what they are feeling. We are there to help them finally complete the process that was interrupted, sometimes decades ago, so that the signal can receive its all-clear and the body can finally, genuinely rest.

> ***Practitioner Note |*** *Clients with significant anxiety often find the prospect of revisiting past events frightening, the body has learned to avoid anything that might activate*

> *the fear response further. Before any Timeline work begins, invest time in establishing safety and explaining exactly what the healing process involves. Make it clear: they are not going back to relive the event. They are going back to finally finish what was left incomplete. The unconscious will not show them anything they cannot handle. And you will be with them the entire time. A quote to remember is, whatever they are fearing the most in the future, they have already emotionally lived through in the past.*

In the session itself, anxiety clients may need more grounding before they can access the Timeline reliably. Slow breathing, feet on the floor, a felt sense of safety in the room — these are not preliminaries to the real work. They are the real work, in its first stage. A nervous system that does not feel safe cannot access the unconscious depth that healing requires. Build the safety first. Everything else follows from that.

After the healing, anxiety clients benefit from understanding what to expect. In the one to three days following a significant release, old emotions can rise to the surface as they complete their processing — what we sometimes call the healing hangover. This is not a sign that something went wrong. It is a sign that something is moving. Preparing clients for this, and offering access to you between sessions if they need it, is an important part of caring for this particular presentation. People with anxiety tend to overthink, and a phone call or message from you that says "this is normal, it means it's working" can be the difference between a client who integrates the healing and one who contracts away from it.

We are not there to calm anxiety down. We are there to help the nervous system finally complete what was interrupted — so that the fear that has been running as present tense for years can finally, fully, become the past.

Depression: When the Energy Turns Inward

Depression is one of the most complex presentations in healing practice, because it can arise from multiple root causes, and the presenting picture often obscures rather than reveals what is actually driving it. In Root-Cause Therapy, we understand depression not as a single thing but as a cluster of possible root causes, each of which requires a somewhat different emphasis in the healing work.

The most common root we encounter is anger that has nowhere to go. Anger is an activating, outward-moving emotion — it is designed to meet a threat, to protect a boundary, to say no to something that is unacceptable. But in many environments, particularly in childhood, anger was not safe to express. It was punished, shamed, or simply met with a response that made clear that this emotion was not permitted. So the anger turned inward. And anger turned inward against the self produces exactly the contraction, the heaviness, the draining of vitality that we recognise as depression. The person is not sad — or not only sad. They are furious, at a level the conscious mind may have no access to, and that fury has nowhere to go but down.

A second common root is unresolved grief — loss that was never fully processed, that sits in the body as a weight the person cannot account for and cannot lift. The loss may be obvious: a bereavement, a relationship ending, a life that did not unfold as hoped. Or it may be less visible: the loss of a childhood that was safe, the loss of a version of the self that never got to exist, the grief of understanding, late in life, what was taken and what was missed.

A third root is chronic nervous system shutdown, the freeze response that follows sustained, inescapable stress. When the survival system has been activated for too long with no resolution, and when fight and flight have not been available as options, the system can simply shut down. Depression as nervous system shutdown presents differently from depression as turned-inward anger — it has a quality of blankness, of flatness, of being behind glass, and it responds well to the slow, gentle, deeply patient approach of building regulation before attempting to access deeper material.

There are other roots too — life circumstances that genuinely do not match the person's needs or values, identity beliefs so entrenched that hope itself feels inaccessible, and in some cases the influence of cultural or social narratives that have made depression feel like an identity rather than an experience. Each client brings their own unique configuration. The Testing Sheet and the sway will show you where to go.

One clinical consideration specific to depression that must be named clearly: if suicidal ideation is present, the first conversation in the first session is about safety. Ask for emergency contact permission. Understand what support systems are in place. Make clear how to reach you between sessions. And work in close collaboration with the client's other treating practitioners — their GP, their psychiatrist if relevant, anyone else who is part of their care. RCT is not a replacement for medical care in this context. It is a complement to it, and the integration of both is the most responsible and the most effective approach.

> ***Practitioner Note |*** *The feedback ratings on the Testing Sheet will often move up and down across the first several sessions with depression clients before they begin to consistently improve. This is normal — as suppressed emotions begin to surface and move, the system can feel temporarily more activated before it settles into something lighter. Prepare clients for this so that a difficult week between sessions does not feel like evidence that healing is not working. It is often the opposite.*

One of the most powerful tools available for depression — once most of the core beliefs have been cleared and the client's self-reported intensity is below five out of ten — is future healing. Depression characteristically closes down the future. The person cannot imagine things being different. They cannot feel forward. A future healing session, where the unconscious takes the client to a version of themselves who has moved through this and is living differently, can break that temporal contraction in a way that nothing in the present can. The future self who has already navigated what the current self cannot imagine navigating becomes a source of felt possibility — not just a concept, but an experience in the body. That experience changes what the nervous system believes is available. And what the nervous system believes is available changes everything.

— — —

Grief: The Many Faces of Loss

Of all the presentations we work with in RCT, grief is the one most people think they understand, and the one that most consistently reveals, in sessions, how much more complex and how much more individual it is than any of our frameworks for it suggest.

When people think of grief, they think of death. And death is indeed where the most acute, most devastating grief arises, particularly the loss of a life partner, a parent, a child, or the person who was the client's only genuine safety in the world. But grief in this work appears in forms that the person themselves may not have named as grief, and part of the practitioner's role is to have the wider frame that allows them to see it.

There is grief for a friendship lost, which carries with it all the insecurities and boundary wounds that the friendship held.

There is pre-grieving, the particular pain of knowing loss is coming, of watching someone you love diminish, of the strange dual time of presence and anticipatory absence. There is the grief that arises in healing work itself, when a client begins to understand their own history clearly enough to feel what it cost them, the childhood they did not have, the relationships they might have had differently, the version of themselves that did not get to exist because of what happened. This grief is real and valid and should never be rushed past. Sometimes simply being witnessed in a space where someone understands what you are grieving is the most therapeutic thing that can happen.

There is complex grief, where a current loss has activated every previous unresolved loss, and the person is not only grieving what is present but everything that was never allowed to be grieved before. And there is the grief of goals and expectations — of a life, a relationship, a family, a self that did not become what was imagined. The could-have-beens that take a person away from what is and trap them in an ache for what was never allowed to happen.

One thing I want to say clearly about grief, because it matters: we are not healing grief so that people forget. We are not helping them move on in the sense of leaving someone behind or diminishing what they meant. What I have witnessed, over and over, is that when grief is truly released, when the emotion is finally allowed to complete — what remains is not absence but love. Gratitude. The ability to remember the wonderful moments without being pulled under by the weight of the loss. The grief was not the love. It was the love that had nowhere to go because the person it was for was no longer there. When the grief moves, the love does not leave. It simply becomes available again — as memory, as warmth, as the quiet awareness of having been shaped by someone who mattered.

We are not healing grief so people can forget. When grief finally completes, what remains is not absence — it is love. The same love, finally free to move.

The protocol for grief follows the standard RCT session structure with a few specific emphases. In the opening conversation, give grief clients more time than usual to speak about what they are carrying — they may have had very few spaces where their loss has been genuinely witnessed rather than managed. In the emotion work, notice that tears arriving when grief is named are almost always an indicator that the emotion has not fully processed — not a sign to stop, but a sign that the body is ready to move something. Make space for that. Hold the space without rushing it.

Note too that the conscious event, the loss the client is most focused on — may not be the root the unconscious surfaces in the healing. An earlier loss, an earlier experience of separation or abandonment or grief unprocessed, may be what is amplifying the current experience. Prepare the client for this possibility before the Timeline work begins, so that it does not confuse or disappoint them when the healing goes somewhere they did not expect.

> ***Practitioner Note |*** *Follow up with grief clients between sessions more consistently than you would with other presentations. A brief message — not a check-in for clinical information, but a genuine human acknowledgement that you are thinking of them — matters enormously to someone who is carrying loss. You do not need to say much. You just need to make clear that they are not navigating this alone.*

— — —

Working With Yourself First

A final word that applies across all three of the presentations in this chapter, and perhaps most urgently here: you cannot hold this work if you have not done it yourself. The practitioner who has never sat with their own grief, who has never let their own anxiety complete rather than suppressing it, who carries their own depression as something managed rather than healed, that practitioner will find, in sessions with these clients, that something in them contracts or avoids at exactly the moments when the deepest presence is needed.

This is not a criticism. It is an invitation, the same invitation this work extends to every client. Go first. Heal your own roots. Not because you must be finished before you can help others, but because every piece of your own healing deepens your capacity to hold another person's. The most effective practitioners of this method are not the most technically skilled. They are the most genuinely present. And genuine presence is the fruit of genuine healing.

Case Study

Client: Sarah B.

The following case demonstrates something that this chapter has pointed toward from the beginning: that anxiety, grief, and the body's symptoms are rarely separate problems requiring separate solutions. Sarah was 35 when she came into our work together. She had chronic hip pain that no physical treatment had been able to resolve, alongside anxiety, chronic stress, and a grief she could not name. The following account describes what four sessions of Root Cause Therapy made possible.

At our first session, Sarah rated her peace at 1 out of 10. Her physical health sat at 2. She was stressed, anxious, and running on very little exercise and too much alcohol. The presenting picture was one of a woman who had been managing for years without ever truly resting — carrying more than she had been given resources to carry, and doing so without complaint.

The testing revealed a complex web of limiting beliefs: "I am not heard," "I cannot meet my own needs," "it is not safe to be vulnerable," "I fear success," "life is hard." Beneath the anxiety and physical pain, what we found was grief — a grief for herself, for the version of her that had learned very early to abandon her own needs in service of others' expectations. The root cause work traced this back to age three, where the earliest imprint of that pattern had formed.

What emerged most powerfully from our sessions was the pattern she described as defining success according to others' definitions rather than her own. She had been rejecting her own sense of what felt right in order to achieve the version of success that external authorities seemed to require. In a pivotal session, she arrived at a recognition that landed with the force of something she had always known but never permitted herself to say: she didn't have to do anything that wasn't right for her. That the bodily sense of rightness — the felt knowledge of what she actually wanted — was trustworthy. That she could speak her truth in the moment, rather than capitulate and carry the resentment of having gone silent again.

By our fourth and final session, Sarah's peace had moved from 1 out of 10 to 10 out of 10. Her anxiety, which had begun at 6, rated at 9 — almost completely resolved. Her physical health had climbed from 2 to 7. She had stopped drinking in the way she had before. She was exercising daily. She had begun yoga. The hip pain, which had been chronic for years, had significantly reduced alongside the emotional release. Her sleep, her energy, her confidence — all transformed.

What Sarah's case demonstrates is something this chapter has returned to repeatedly: anxiety, grief, and physical symptoms are not separate compartments. They are expressions of the same unresolved material, stored in the body, waiting for the conditions that allow them to finally complete. When we found the root — the moment at age three when a child first learned that her feelings were not safe to express — the resolution rippled outward into every domain of her life simultaneously. That is what root-cause work makes possible.

— RCT Certified Practitioner, Alena Turley

Peace from 1 to 10 in four sessions. That number is striking, and it matters. But what it represents is more important than the number itself: a woman who came in unable to rest, unable to grieve, unable to trust her own body — leaving with access to a quality of presence with herself that no amount of symptom management had been able to provide. This is what it looks like when anxiety and grief are approached not as problems to be managed, but as messengers pointing toward something that was interrupted long ago and is finally, in the safety of this work, able to complete.

In the next chapter, we turn to addiction — one of the most misunderstood, most stigmatised, and most treatable presentations in healing practice when approached through the root-cause lens.

Reflection

Do you have a healthy relationship with the full spectrum of your emotions — or do you tend to suppress, manage, or move past certain feelings before they've been fully felt? Which emotions are hardest to sit with?

Your reflection:

— — —

Chapter Seventeen: Addiction and Compulsion

In Root-Cause Therapy, we understand addiction as a trauma response, a coping mechanism, a way of feeling okay when the person does not know how to process their uncomfortable feelings, emotions, and flashbacks. When the nervous system is carrying unbearable pain and has never been given the tools to process it, and when something is discovered that provides even temporary relief, a substance, a behaviour, a pattern, the brain encodes that discovery powerfully. It burns it in as a solution, because the nervous system is always, always trying to help us survive. The addiction is not the problem. It is the person's best available answer to the problem. And the problem is pain.

Dr. Gabor Maté, whose work on trauma and addiction is among the most[15,16] important of our time, puts it simply and precisely: the question is never "why the addiction?" but "why the pain?" Once we understand that the addiction is an attempt to solve the problem — not the problem itself, the entire therapeutic orientation changes. We stop trying to remove the coping mechanism. We start healing what it was coping from.

The question is never "why the addiction?" but "why the pain?" The addiction is not the problem — it is the person's best available answer to the problem. Heal the pain, and the answer is no longer needed. — Dr. Gabor Maté

My Own Journey With Addiction

I write this chapter not as someone who has observed addiction from a distance and developed theories about it, but as someone who has lived it. My own experience with addiction began when I was fourteen years old.

My mother had just left a domestic violence situation, with two young children and me, a young teenager who did not know how to process what I had witnessed and what I was carrying. I had never been taught to feel my emotions, let alone move them through me. I had no language for the fear, the grief, the shame, the constant hypervigilance of a child who had grown up in an environment that was not safe. What I had was a nervous system flooded with unprocessed pain, and no tools to metabolise it.

When I found something that gave me a sense of peace, ease, and confidence — states I could not access naturally because of what was stored in my body, the signal it burned into my nervous system was powerful. This works. When you feel like that, do this. That is not a moral failure. That is a nervous system finding what it needs to survive.

What changed everything was not willpower. It was not hitting rock bottom and deciding to be different. It was the first healing session I ever received, the session that created the bridge between my conscious and my unconscious, that showed me for the first time the actual root of the patterns I was living from. In that session, my addictions reduced almost immediately. Not because I had decided to stop. Because for the first time, the nervous system had been given something that actually addressed what it was coping from. The need for the coping mechanism reduced because the pain beneath it had begun, finally, to move.

That experience is the foundation of everything in this chapter. Not theory. Lived understanding, from the inside.

— — —

What We Are Actually Working With

Addiction takes many forms — substances, relationships, food, work, social media, gambling, sex, and while some carry greater physical risk than others, the underlying mechanism is consistent across all of them. Something that produces a neurochemical state the person cannot access through ordinary means has been encoded as a solution to emotional pain. And the more adverse childhood experiences a person carries, the research consistently shows, the more likely they are to develop some form of addiction. Not because ACEs predetermine addiction, but because the pain accumulates, the nervous system's regulation capacity is compromised, and the search for relief becomes increasingly urgent.

Shame and guilt deserve particular attention here, because they sit at the very lowest frequencies on the emotional spectrum, the heaviest, most contracting, most paralysing of all emotions, and they operate in a vicious cycle with addiction. The addiction produces shame. The shame produces more pain. The pain produces more need for the coping mechanism. The coping mechanism produces more shame. Breaking this cycle requires addressing both dimensions simultaneously — healing the root traumas that generated the pain the addiction was managing, and directly releasing the shame and guilt accumulated through the addiction itself, without ever adding to that burden through judgement.

This means that the most essential quality a practitioner brings to addiction work is not knowledge or technique. It is the complete and unconditional absence of shame. If a client senses, at any level, that you are judging them — for what they have used, for how much, for what they have done while in active addiction, for having relapsed — they will contract away from the healing rather than toward it. Your session room must be the safest place they have ever been allowed to exist with this part of themselves. That safety is not a nice-to-have. It is the therapeutic foundation without which nothing else can reach what needs to be reached.

It also helps to understand what addiction actually is — at its most fundamental level — before any technique is applied. What we are addicted to is never really the substance or the behaviour. It is the feeling. The sense of peace. The relief from anxiety. The warmth that feels like love. The confidence that ordinarily feels out of reach. The sense, even briefly, of being okay in one's own skin. Every addiction, regardless of its surface form, is an attempt to access a state that the person cannot reach naturally, and the reason they cannot reach it naturally is almost always rooted in what their early experiences taught the nervous system about whether those states were safe or available.

Here is what I want practitioners to hold clearly, because it changes everything about how you sit with a client carrying addiction: the chemicals that produce those states, the warmth, the peace, the sense of connection and worth — are not external. They are already inside the person. Dopamine, serotonin, oxytocin, endorphins — these are not manufactured by substances. Substances only manipulate the pathways through which those chemicals are already released. The person is not broken. They are not lacking something they were never given. They are blocked from something they already have. And the root-cause work is not about adding something new to the system. It is about removing what is in the way of the system reaching what was always there.

This reframe — from deficiency to blockage — is one of the most important things you can offer a client who has spent years being told, or telling themselves, that they are fundamentally broken. They are not broken. Their system found the only available route to something it genuinely needed. When the root causes that blocked the natural route are healed, the substance no longer has to do the work. Not because the person has finally mustered enough willpower or self-discipline. Because the need is being met another way.

> **Practitioner Note |** *When a client relapses between sessions, and with addiction work, this will happen — do not approach it with concern or disappointment, however subtle. Approach it with genuine curiosity and even enthusiasm: a relapse is information. It has shown you another trigger, another root that is ready to be addressed. Treat it as the gift it is, a specific, concrete point of entry into material that might otherwise have taken much longer to surface. The client who tells you about a relapse is trusting you with something tender. Receive it that way.*

A Different Approach: Not Abstinence, But Root-Cause Healing

The approach we take at The Centre for Healing has never been abstinence-based. We do not require clients to have detoxed before working with us, or to have committed to stopping before we begin. We work with them in their current life, in their current environment, with the current relationships and triggers and circumstances that are present because that is where the actual healing needs to happen.

The reason for this is both philosophical and practical. Philosophically, asking someone to stop their primary coping mechanism before you have given them anything to replace it with is asking the nervous system to become defenceless before it has been given a new form of regulation. It does not work, and when it fails, it generates more shame. Practically, the triggers that are driving the addiction are in the person's actual life — in specific relationships, environments, moments of stress or loneliness or shame. Working with those triggers as they arise, in real time across sessions, is more precise and more effective than working in a protected bubble.

This approach does mean that clients may use their substance or engage in their behaviour during the period of working with you. That is expected. What you will typically observe, as the root work progresses, is that the frequency and intensity naturally reduce — not because the client is trying harder to stop, but because the need for the coping mechanism is genuinely decreasing as the pain beneath it is healed. The relief that only the addiction could previously provide begins to become available through natural regulation as the nervous system's baseline shifts. And when that happens, when peace and ease and confidence become accessible without the substance, the choice to continue or not looks genuinely different.

What we observed at The Centre for Healing, with clients whose addictions ranged from alcohol to ice (methamphetamines), was something that still strikes me as one of the most compelling demonstrations of this work's efficacy. A client arrives with an emotional baseline sitting somewhere in the lower register of the Scale of Consciousness — in the territory of shame, grief, apathy, or chronic fear. Their substance of choice provides a temporary lift, moving them up the scale toward something that feels, briefly, like relief or connection or ease. Then the effect wears off, the baseline crashes back, and the pull to use again is simply the nervous system seeking to return to the only elevated state it has access to. This is not weakness. It is mathematics. The substance is working. It is just not working sustainably.

As the root work progresses and the stored emotional charge beneath the addiction begins to clear, the client's baseline rises. Not dramatically, not all at once — but measurably, session by session. And then something remarkable happens that we witnessed repeatedly in our clinic: clients would try their substance again, fully expecting the familiar lift, and find that it no longer worked the way it once did. More than that — it pulled them down. A substance that had previously provided temporary elevation now produced discomfort, flatness, or a hangover that felt worse than before. Because the baseline had risen. The gap between their natural state and the effect of the substance had narrowed. And for some, it had reversed. In those cases, we did not need to motivate the client to stop, or work on their willpower, or create accountability structures around abstinence. They stopped because the substance was no longer doing what they needed it to do. Healing the root had changed the mathematics entirely.

From Survival to Expansion

How healing raises the baseline — and why the need for coping mechanisms naturally falls away

	The Healing Journey	Polyvagal State & Nervous System
ntenı 700+ Peace 600 Joy 540 PANI Love 500 easo 400	**Expanded Consciousness — Life Beyond Survival** · Love, willingness and acceptance become the natural felt sense · Awareness extends outward: self — family — community — world · Thoughts shift from scarcity and threats to contribution and meaning · Creativity, connection and purpose replace survival as motivators · Generational patterns stop here — children inherit peace, not trauma · Global wellbeing becomes a natural expression of inner wholeness	**VENTRAL VAGAL — Social Engagement** · Safety, connection, curiosity, openness · Present-moment awareness & play · Compassion, creativity, genuine rest · Healthy attachment & attunement · The nervous system destination of RCT
	ıe rises. Substance no longer works — need dissolves	
epta 350 lingn 310 POW utral 250 ourag 200	**Root-Cause Therapy — Raising the Baseline** · Stored emotional charges resolved at the original root event · Nervous system learns safety for the first time — ventral vagal · Baseline rises measurably, session by session · The relief the substance provided becomes internally accessible · No willpower required — the need itself gently dissolves · Coping mechanisms are no longer doing their job; healing is	**SYMPATHETIC — Fight / Flight** · Hyperarousal, anxiety, anger, panic · Survival mode — danger perceived · Relational capacity significantly reduced · Addiction temporarily reduces this activation · RCT resolves what keeps the system locked here
	☒ Addiction temporarily lifts to here — then crashes b	
Pride 175 Ange 150 Desire 125 FORC Fear 100 Grief 75 path 50	**Addiction & Coping — Borrowed Relief** · Substance or behaviour temporarily lifts the baseline to desire, courage, even joy · Provides the only available access to ease and connection · Feelings never learned to generate from within — never taught how · This is not weakness. It is mathematics: the substance is working · When the effect wears off, the baseline crashes — the cycle repeats	**DORSAL VAGAL — Freeze / Collapse** · Shutdown, numbness, dissociation · Shame, apathy, deep hopelessness · Deepest trauma baseline state · Immune, digestive, social systems impaired · Addiction temporarily lifts from here
Guilt 30 TRAU ham 20	**Low Baseline — Unresolved Trauma** · Shame, guilt, grief, fear dominate the daily felt sense · Nervous system locked in survival — fight, flight, or freeze · No safe attachment modelled. Emotions not permitted or taught. · No co-regulation available. The world feels threatening. · Consciousness contracted — focused entirely on self-survival	**Collapsed Baseline — Early Trauma** · Chronic survival state from childhood · No safe adult to co-regulate with · Emotions not taught, not processed · Nervous system never learned safety · World experienced as threat, not home

From Survival to Expansion — how healing raises the baseline and why the need for coping mechanisms naturally falls away.

We do not claim to cure addiction. We heal the emotional and unconscious roots that are driving it, and we trust that as those roots are addressed, the system naturally reorganises toward what is genuinely nourishing rather than what is temporarily numbing. For many clients, across the three months or more of consistent work that this typically requires, that reorganisation is profound and lasting.

Working With Addiction in Sessions

The session structure for addiction work follows the standard RCT framework with several important adaptations. In the initial consultation, use the Scale of Consciousness to give the client a tangible picture of where they currently are emotionally, and where the substance or behaviour takes them — momentarily up the scale, but always crashing back below the starting point. This simple map helps many clients understand, perhaps for the first time, the mechanism they are caught in without any judgement attached to it.

As you work through the Testing Sheet, do not make the addiction the primary focus of the session. The addiction is the presenting symptom. The session's focus is the emotional pain, the trauma, the limiting beliefs that are driving it. When you reach the monitoring section of the sheet, note the frequency and intensity of the addictive behaviour as data to track session by session — but hold it lightly, not as the measure of success.

In the belief work, the standard Testing Sheet beliefs will surface relevant material, and several specific custom beliefs are worth adding for addiction presentations. Beliefs such as I cannot relax without the substance, I cannot have fun without it, I am a user, I am ashamed — these carry the identity dimension of addiction that can be as binding as the neurochemical one. When a person has organised their sense of self around the addiction, clearing the identity beliefs is as important as clearing the trauma roots.

In the past healing, you can approach from several angles depending on what the sway identifies as most ready. You can ask directly for the root cause of the addiction, the first event which, when healed, will reduce or remove the need for it. You can work on the specific traumas that predated and precipitated the addiction's beginning. You can address the earliest experience with the substance itself, releasing any positive emotional charge that was encoded at that moment because sometimes what is most strongly encoded is not the pain the addiction was managing but the relief it first provided, and that encoded relief needs to be gently cleared.

Shame and guilt accumulated through the addiction, the things done, said, or left undone while in active use — become their own healing focus once the earlier roots have been substantially addressed. This is tender work, and it needs to be approached after trust and therapeutic rapport are well established, never before.

> ***Practitioner Note |** Some clients will not disclose all of their addictions in early sessions. This is not deception — it is the natural protection of material that carries the most shame. Trust that it will emerge as the relationship deepens and as earlier work demonstrates that this is genuinely a safe space. Never push for full disclosure before the client is ready. The material will come when the system feels secure enough to bring it.*

The Void and What Fills It

One thing that consistently catches clients by surprise in addiction recovery work, and that practitioners need to be prepared to hold — is the void that appears as the addiction begins to lose its grip. When a pattern that has organised a person's daily life, their social world, their sense of identity, and their emotional regulation for years begins to shift, what is left in its place is not immediately comfortable. It can feel like emptiness. Like loss. Like not knowing who they are without it.

This is a critical juncture, and it needs to be named and normalised before it arrives rather than after. The void is not a sign that something has gone wrong. It is the space being created for something new — for the person's actual self, their real preferences, their genuine capacity for joy and connection and regulation, to emerge. But the space can feel frightening before it feels like freedom, and a client who is not prepared for it may interpret it as evidence that the healing is not working or that they are somehow worse without the addiction than with it.

Once most of the limiting beliefs have been cleared and the person's own reported emotional baseline has improved significantly, future healing becomes one of the most powerful tools available. Taking the client forward to meet a version of themselves who has moved through this, who has found genuine purpose, genuine connection, genuine peace that does not depend on anything external — gives the nervous system a felt destination. Not an abstract hope. An experienced possibility. And what the nervous system has experienced as possible, it will work toward.

The families of people with addiction also deserve acknowledgement here. They are in pain too — carrying their own fear, their own helplessness, their own grief for the person they love and the relationship they have with them. Offering sessions, or referring family members to another RCT practitioner, is one of the most meaningful things you can do, both for the family members themselves and for the healing environment of the person you are working with. Recovery does not happen in isolation. It happens in relationship. And healing the relationships around the addiction is part of healing the addiction itself.

— — —

This work with addiction is among the most demanding and the most rewarding in all of healing practice. The client who arrives carrying years of shame, years of failed attempts, years of being told they are the problem, and who discovers, across months of genuine root-cause work, that the system that drove all of it was not a moral failure but a faithful response to unbearable pain, that client's liberation is something I have had the privilege of witnessing many times. And each time, it moves me in the same way.

Because what is revealed, as the addiction and its roots are healed, is not a damaged person who has finally managed their disease. It is a whole person who was always there beneath it — waiting, with extraordinary patience, for someone to finally ask the right question. Not "why the addiction?" but "what were you trying to feel?" and "what happened that made that feeling so necessary?" and "what would your life look like if you no longer needed it?"

That life is available. This work makes it possible. And you, as a practitioner who approaches addiction with understanding rather than judgement and with root-cause precision rather than symptom management, are one of the people who can help someone find their way there.

Reflection

> *Do you see anywhere in your life where you reach for something — a substance, a behaviour, a distraction, a person — as a coping mechanism, something that you are afraid or defensive about stopping or giving up completely?*

Your reflection:

Chapter Eighteen: My Own Healing

The first is about sexual trauma. The second is about Ryan — my partner, the co-founder of The Centre for Healing, and the person who taught me something essential about healing that I could not have learned any other way.

I share these not because I believe practitioners are obligated to make themselves transparent in this way. They are not. I share them because I want you to understand, as fully as I can communicate it, what this work actually does when it reaches the places that matter most. And because the two stories together say something I have not been able to say as directly anywhere else in this book: healing is not a destination you arrive at once. It is something you return to, again and again, as life gives you new material to bring to it. The creator of a method is not exempt from needing it. The person who teaches healing is not finished with their own.

The Story I Did Not Know How to Tell

As far back as I can remember, I was hypervigilant around men. Not in a way I could name or explain — just a low-level watchfulness that lived in my body, a constant awareness of where people were in a room, of whether I was being seen. As a teenager, I wondered if something had happened to me that I couldn't consciously access. The hypervigilance was real, but I had no story to attach it to.

Then, when I was fourteen, I went to a party with friends. I found myself alone with a man who was about fifteen years older than me. I froze. He forced me onto a basketball court and sexually abused me.

In the years that followed, I became very promiscuous. I could not explain it at the time — I told myself I simply had a high sex drive, that this was just who I was. But the pattern had a feeling underneath it that I could not quite touch. A compulsive quality. A reaching for something that never quite landed.

When I eventually did my own healing work through RCT, what emerged went deeper than the event at fourteen. In a past-life regression, I encountered a lifetime in which I had been sexually abused as a child by my father. That past-life imprint was the root of the hypervigilance I had carried since childhood, the watchfulness, the sensitivity around men, the feeling of danger that arrived before any conscious thought. When the assault at fourteen happened in this life, it landed on top of that earlier wound, adding another layer to what the nervous system already believed was true: that the body was not safe, that intimacy was dangerous, that I needed to manage and control what happened to me before someone else did.

What I came to understand in the healing, as we traced the timeline back and then forward again, was that the promiscuity had never been about desire. It was trauma reenactment. My nervous system had been running a programme, over and over again, trying to find its way back to power — trying to reclaim, through repetition, what had been taken from it in that moment at fourteen. Not consciously. Not deliberately. Simply faithfully, the way nervous systems do.

When that root was healed, when the past-life material was addressed and the fourteen-year-old was given the experience of safety and agency she had been denied — something simply settled. The drive that had felt compulsive quietly released. I found that I could be monogamous without effort, that intimacy felt different in my body, that the patterns that had controlled so much of my behaviour for years had lost their grip. Not because I changed my thinking. Because something had shifted at the level where the pattern actually lived.

I share this because I want practitioners working with sexual trauma to understand what their clients are actually navigating. The behaviour that looks problematic, the promiscuity, the shutdown, the patterns in relationships that make no rational sense — is almost always the nervous system's best available attempt to manage an unprocessed wound. It is not a character flaw. It is not a failure of willpower or self-awareness. It is the system doing exactly what systems do: protecting, adapting, trying to find its way back to safety through the only routes it knows. That knowledge, held with genuine compassion rather than clinical detachment, changes how you sit with a client carrying this material. And that change, though subtle, is felt.

What I can say, in the space before your words arrive here, is this: sexual trauma is among the most isolating of all wounds, because it is so rarely spoken aloud. It carries shame that does not belong to the person who survived it, and that shame compounds in silence — growing heavier with every year it is not named, not witnessed, not given the space it needs to finally move.

When I eventually brought this material to my own healing work, what I encountered was not just the events themselves but the entire architecture that had been built around them, the beliefs, the protective patterns, the ways I had learned to manage and contain and move around a wound that had never been directly addressed. The healing did not happen in one session. It happened in layers, over time, with a trust in the process that had to be rebuilt at each new layer as the unconscious revealed what was next.

What emerged on the other side was not the absence of what had happened. What had happened remained exactly as it was, a fact, a part of the history. What changed was the weight of it. And the ways it had been silently shaping decisions, reactions, and relationships that I had never connected to it consciously. When those connections were healed at the root, the shape of my life shifted in ways I had not known to expect.

I share this because I want practitioners reading this book to understand, from the inside, what your clients who carry sexual trauma are navigating when they sit across from you. The courage it takes to begin. The patience the healing requires. The particular care this territory demands — not just clinically, but humanly. You are not just a technician working with a presenting symptom. You are a witness. And witnessing, done well, is itself a form of healing.

The most important thing I learned from my own sexual trauma healing is that the shame was never mine. It took going to the root to know that in my body, not just in my head. That distinction — between knowing something and knowing it in your body — is the entire reason this work exists.

— — —

The Time Ryan Asked Me to Stop

I have always thrown myself into healing. When I understood what this work could do, I wanted to do as much of it as possible, as quickly as possible. More sessions, deeper dives, more beliefs uncovered and resolved. I had a name for it eventually: belief mining. Healing for the sake of healing, chasing every block without pause, as though the faster we cleared, the sooner everything would be free.

Ryan, who had been doing his own deep work alongside me, and who, in the early years, embraced it with the same commitment — eventually reached a point where he needed to stop. Not stop permanently. Just stop for now. He asked me, clearly and plainly: please, can we have a break from healing?

I had to sit with that. My instinct was to keep going. But what his request was pointing to was something I had not yet fully understood: that the nervous system needs time between sessions. Not because healing is not working — but precisely because it is. When we go into deep material, when long-suppressed trauma begins to move and release, the body enters a process that does not end when the session ends. Neurological pathways are rewiring. Old stress is leaving the tissues. Emotions that have been held tightly for years are, at last, being allowed to complete. This takes energy. It takes time. It is real physiological work.

We call it the healing hangover. After a deep session, a client may feel tired for days. They may feel emotionally tender, more sensitive than usual, moved easily to tears or to irritability. Their sleep may shift. Old feelings may surface briefly before they pass. This is not a sign that something has gone wrong. It is a sign that the system is doing exactly what it is supposed to do: integrating, consolidating, becoming flexible in ways it could not be before. It is beautiful work. But it requires rest, and it requires space, and it cannot be rushed.

What Ryan taught me, by asking for that break, was the difference between belief mining and intentional healing. RCT is not a practice of clearing as many blocks as possible as fast as possible. It is a practice of healing with a purpose — addressing specific root causes in service of a specific shift in a person's life, and then giving the system the time it needs to integrate that shift before the next layer is approached. Sessions paced fortnightly or monthly are often not just reasonable — they are ideal. The depth of a single RCT session is such that some clients genuinely describe it as equivalent to years of conventional therapy. That kind of depth demands proportional integration time.

I carry this now into how I work with clients and into how I train practitioners. Always ask: what does this person's system actually need right now? Sometimes it is to go deeper. Sometimes it is to pause and let what has already happened settle. The goal was never the maximum amount of healing in the minimum amount of time. The goal has always been lasting change, and lasting change requires a nervous system that has been given the grace of its own natural rhythm.

Who is being affected? Is there support available between sessions, or is the client returning to an environment that does not understand what they are going through? And, particularly for practitioners who are in their own intensive healing work — what is the impact of that process on the people you share your life with? These are not peripheral questions. They are central to how we care well for ourselves and for the people we love while doing this work.

— — —

What Personal Stories Are For

I debated, in the writing of this book, how much of myself to include. There are books written by practitioners who maintain a clear professional distance, who write about the method, the science, the cases, without ever making themselves personally visible. That is a valid choice, and it has integrity.

But I am not that kind of writer, and this is not that kind of book. Root-Cause Therapy was built from lived experience — mine, Ryan's, and the many practitioners and clients who have shaped it through the decade of The Centre for Healing. The method emerged from the questions that real pain asked and from the answers that real healing provided. To write about it without including the personal dimension would be to strip something essential from its character.

More than that: I believe that practitioners who share carefully chosen pieces of their own story, who have done enough of their own healing to be able to hold it without it bleeding into the room — are more effective practitioners. Not because clients need to know everything about your history. They do not. But because having been to the places you are guiding others toward changes how you navigate the territory. You know it from the inside. You know what it costs. You know what it gives back. And that knowing communicates itself, without words, in every session.

In the next chapter, we turn from my stories to two client stories — cases that have stayed with me because of what they revealed about the reach of this work into territory that most conventional approaches have rarely been able to touch.

— — —

Reflection

> *Is there a story from your own life — something that shaped you deeply — that you have never fully told, or never fully let yourself feel? What has it been waiting for?*

Your reflection:

— — —

PART FIVE — PERSONAL STORIES

Chapter Nineteen: When the Work Reaches Further

Both clients have given permission for their stories to be shared. Both have been anonymised. Both changed what I believed was possible.

The Love Chemical: Healing a Heroin Addiction at Its Root

He came in presenting what he described simply as a heroin dependency. He was functional, in the sense that he was still holding his life together — work, relationships, an outer surface that largely concealed the extent of what was happening underneath. But the dependency had been growing for years, and he had tried the conventional routes. Rehab. Abstinence programmes. Substitution therapy. Each had produced temporary results. None had addressed what he was beginning to suspect was the actual problem.

What he suspected, and what the RCT process confirmed in the first session — was that the heroin was not producing a high in the conventional sense. It was producing something that felt, in his body, remarkably like love. The warm, flooding sense of being held and safe and deeply connected that the drug delivered was not something he had been able to access naturally. And when we began to explore why, the story that emerged was one of early relational deprivation so consistent and so complete that the nervous system had essentially no template for what genuine safety and connection felt like — except through the drug.

Several sessions in, after we had addressed the earliest attachment wounds, the specific experiences in which the need for safety and connection had first gone unmet — we introduced a future session. Rather than continuing to work backwards through the past, we guided the client forward, into an imagined point in his life where he was living without the dependency. A future self who had access to everything the heroin had been providing.

What happened in that session stopped me.

For the first time in his life, the client was able to feel maternal love. Not as an idea, not as something he had read about or observed in others, but as a felt experience in his own body. A warmth. A sense of being held and welcomed and genuinely wanted. He had never felt it before — not in his childhood, not in any relationship that had come after. The only time anything close to it had been available to him was through the drug.

And now it was there. Inside him. Accessible without the substance.

This is what I want practitioners to understand about what we carry in our bodies: the chemicals that produce the experience of love, safety, and connection are not external. They are ours. They are already in us, the capacity for warmth, for tenderness, for the felt sense of being held by life. But when developmental trauma or relational deprivation has shaped the nervous system from early on, the pathways to those internal states can be blocked so completely that a person does not know they exist. They have never had access to them. And so when a substance or a behaviour opens a door to something that feels like those states — however artificially, however temporarily — of course it becomes something the system holds onto fiercely. It is providing the only experience of home the nervous system has ever known.

Once the client had accessed that state from the inside, the grip of the dependency began to shift. Not because he had made a decision or deployed willpower. Because the need the heroin had been meeting was, for the first time, being met another way.

What struck me most in this work, and what I want practitioners to hold when they encounter addiction of any kind — was how completely the substance made sense once we understood what it was providing. The nervous system had found the one thing that could deliver, even artificially and temporarily, the experience it had been seeking since childhood. Of course the dependency was profound. Of course willpower alone could not touch it. The nervous system was not making an irrational choice. It was meeting a fundamental human need through the only available pathway.

The healing that followed addressed the root of that need, the experiences that had made genuine connection feel unavailable, the beliefs that had formed around those experiences, the inner child work that brought the adult self back to the child who had learned to survive without the safety every child deserves. It was not quick. It required sustained work across multiple sessions and a depth of patience and presence from the therapeutic relationship that matched the depth of the wound.

The work across this case spanned several months. The early sessions focused on the relational trauma, the specific experiences of absence, unpredictability, and emotional unavailability that had shaped his internal world from the beginning. Each session addressed a layer. Each layer revealed the next. And the pattern of his relationship to the substance shifted gradually but unmistakably as the roots were addressed: the urgency softened, the frequency reduced, the psychological grip loosened in ways that none of the programmes he had previously engaged had been able to produce.

There was no single dramatic turning point — or rather, the future session was the pivot, but what made it possible was everything that had been cleared before it. By the time his nervous system was able to access that state of warmth and safety from the inside, enough of the historical material had been addressed that there was space in the system to receive it. He was not the same person he had been at the start of the work. And the dependency, deprived of the need it had been filling, no longer had the same claim on him.

The last I heard from him, he was living without the substance. Not white-knuckling an abstinence. Not managing a craving through willpower or distraction. Simply living, with access to a warmth inside himself that he had not known was there, and no longer needing the drug to take him somewhere his own body could now reach.

What this case gave me was a lasting reorientation of how I understand the relationship between addiction and love. Not every dependency has this character, the presentations are as individual as the people carrying them. But the question is always worth asking, underneath the specific substance or behaviour: what is this providing that the person has not been able to access in any other way? What fundamental need is it meeting? And what would need to heal for that need to begin to be met differently?

The question beneath every addiction is the same: what is this providing that nothing else has been able to give? When you find the honest answer to that question, you find the root. And when you heal the root, the provision is no longer needed.

More Than a Label: Healing Behind a Diagnosis

The second case is a man I will call D — in his early fifties, referred through a GP, and carrying a diagnosis of ADHD that he had held for a significant portion of his adult life. He had been on medication for years. It worked, in the sense that it helped him function. But he had begun to wonder, in the way people do when they have managed a condition rather than addressed it, whether there was something underneath the label that had never been looked at.

Before I go further: a note on working with adults with ADHD diagnoses, and why RCT is appropriate for this population. The method is designed for adults whose prefrontal cortex, the part of the brain responsible for executive function, impulse regulation, and conscious self-awareness — is fully formed. That development is typically complete around the age of twenty-one. This matters clinically because the semi-conscious regression work of RCT requires the client to remain sufficiently present and self-aware to engage critically with what emerges — to accept or reject a framing, to find their own learning, rather than having one imposed. A fully formed prefrontal cortex is what makes that safety possible. It is why RCT, in its primary form, is an adult methodology.

With D, what the sessions revealed over time was not a neurological malfunction but a nervous system that had learned — through specific early experiences, that stillness was unsafe. That settling into the present moment left him exposed in ways that had once felt genuinely dangerous. The hyperactivity of attention, the inability to focus, the constant scanning and movement — these were not random symptoms. They were a programme the system had installed to keep him safe. And the system had been running that programme, faithfully and without interruption, for decades.

We worked session by session, not on the diagnosis but on the root causes of each symptom and belief as they surfaced. The difficulty concentrating. The sense of being fundamentally different, somehow wrong. The deep exhaustion of a life spent managing rather than resting. Each belief pointed to something earlier. Each earlier something pointed to a moment at which the nervous system had made a decision about what was required to survive.

Over approximately three months of sessions, something began to shift that the medication alone had never produced. D began to notice that he could settle. Not always, not immediately — but there were moments of genuine presence that felt qualitatively different from anything he had experienced before. His self-care changed without effort. His capacity to focus improved, not through discipline but through a reduction in the underlying activation that had been fragmenting his attention for as long as he could remember.

Working in close communication with his GP throughout, D gradually and carefully began to reduce his medication. The tapering was slow, guided medically, and done in full awareness that this was his choice and his process — not a goal we had set. What made it possible was not that RCT had cured a neurological condition. It is that the root cause material driving many of the symptoms had been addressed, and the system, no longer running the same survival programme at the same intensity, no longer needed the same level of external support to function.

I want to be precise here, because this territory requires precision: RCT does not treat ADHD. It does not treat any diagnosis. What it does is address the root cause material that may be contributing to how a diagnosis presents in a specific person, and in doing so, it can change what that person's system needs. Sometimes significantly. D's outcome was his own. It will not be universal. But what his case demonstrated, as clearly as any I have witnessed, is the difference between managing a label and actually addressing the human being underneath it.

— — —

What These Stories Are Asking of You

I share these cases not as evidence that RCT can heal anything, or as marketing for a method. I share them because they illustrate something I have come to hold as a central conviction across a decade of this work: the presenting symptom is almost never the whole story. Almost never.

The heroin dependency was a love story, a nervous system's faithful attempt to find what it had never been given. The ADHD was a survival programme, a persons intelligence expressing itself through the only available channel. Neither could be adequately addressed at the level of the symptom, because neither originated there.

When you sit with a client — any client, with any presentation, and you hold the question "what is this communicating, and what would need to heal for it to no longer need to communicate this way?" you are doing something that the majority of therapeutic approaches do not do. You are treating the person as a whole, coherent, intelligent system whose responses always make sense in the context of what they have experienced. And that act of genuine, curious, non-pathologising regard — before any technique is applied — is itself a form of healing.

Because many of the people who come to this work have spent years being treated as the problem rather than as the person. As the diagnosis rather than the human being underneath it. As the symptom rather than the story the symptom is trying to tell.

You are not just a practitioner of a method. You are a person who sees differently, who looks at what others have labelled and asks the question that changes everything: where did this begin, and what has it been trying to say?

In Part Six, we turn to the practical — how to build a practice from this foundation, how to find clients, how to sustain yourself in this work, and how to contribute to the wider healing that the world so urgently needs.

— — —

Reflection

> *Is there a pattern or belief in your life that has persisted through everything you've tried — something that, if it were finally resolved at the root, would change the shape of your whole life?*

Your reflection:

— — —

PART SIX

Building Your Practice

Chapter Twenty: The Courage to Begin

It is imposter syndrome. And it visits almost every new RCT practitioner I have ever trained, without exception, including the ones who go on to build the most extraordinary practices. Including me.

My Own Beginning

When I first began offering sessions as a practitioner — before The Centre for Healing existed, before the training program, before any of the infrastructure that now surrounds this work — I was doing it from my apartment , with a handful of clients who had come to me largely through my social media, as I had excitedly shared my story of transformation and what I had studied recently. I believed in the method completely. I had experienced its effects in my own life in ways that were undeniable. I had seen it work in the practice sessions during training.

And yet, sitting across from a real client with a real wound and a real hope that I might be able to help — I was terrified. Not because I did not know what to do. I did know what to do. The terror was older than that and more fundamental: the fear that I was not enough for this. That someone would find out that I was not really qualified for the weight of what they were bringing. That the gap between who I needed to be and who I actually was would be discovered, probably in the session, probably at the worst possible moment.

That fear had a root cause. Of course it did. I eventually went to that root, the beliefs about my own competence and worth that had formed early and had been quietly running my professional life from underneath for years. When I healed those roots, something changed. Not that the fear disappeared entirely — but it lost its grip. It stopped being the thing that decided what I would and would not attempt.

My first experience of this kind of work was not in a training room. It was as a client. I had gone to see a coach who was working with something that resembled RCT in some ways — regression work, belief clearing, emotional release — though it was missing much of what I would later come to understand as essential. What brought me there was not trauma, exactly. It was patterns. Specifically, repeating patterns in my romantic life that I could not explain and could not seem to stop. The same dynamics, the same endings, the same feeling that something was wrong with me in ways I could not name or fix.

Something shifted in that session. Enough that when the practitioner mentioned they offered training, I said yes without hesitation. I was working a full-time corporate job at the time. I had been for years, the structured hours, the performance metrics, the fluorescent-lit predictability of it. It was fine. It was not mine. I dreaded Mondays in the way I think a lot of people dread Mondays — not because anything terrible was happening, but because nothing that was supposed to matter actually did. I used to watch my dad come home on a Friday and say he could not wait for Monday. He loved his work that much. I had spent years quietly wondering if that was something that happened to other people.

Halfway through the training, I stopped wondering.

There is no other way to describe what happened except that it felt like a lightning bolt. I was sitting in the room, in the middle of a session, and something landed in my chest with a clarity I had never felt before: this is it. This is what I am supposed to be doing. I knew I was meant to be in business — I had always known that, somewhere. I knew I was meant to be helping people. I had simply never found the intersection of those two things before. There it was.

And then, almost immediately, the fear arrived.

What if I fail? What will people think? The shame of trying something this different, this outside what I was supposed to be doing, and not being good enough for it. The blocks came in fast and they came in hard. I could feel them in my body, the tightening, the retreat, the familiar voice that had been with me for as long as I could remember telling me that I was not the kind of person this happened for.

We did the work. In one of the sessions during the training, I went back to a memory from school, a moment when I had done something wrong, made a mistake, been seen to get it wrong in front of others. It seemed small in isolation. It was not small in what it had produced. That moment had become evidence for a belief I had been carrying ever since, quietly and completely, without ever having named it: that I was stupid. That I was not capable of the kind of intelligence that real success required. I had been living from underneath that belief for my entire adult life, and I had not known it was there.

When we cleared it, when I went to the root of that moment and the child in it was finally given the truth rather than the wound — something reorganised. I reconnected with an intelligence I had been disconnected from since that day at school. An innate knowing that I had always had and had simply been unable to access. And with it came a different relationship to failure entirely: I realised I could not fail. Not in the way the fear was describing. I had found my purpose. And a person who has found their purpose cannot fail — they can only keep going, imperfectly and persistently, toward the thing they were made for.

That was about twelve years ago. Within weeks of completing the training, I resigned from my corporate job. I have not looked back once.

I share this not because my story is universal — it is not. But because I want every practitioner reading this to know that the fear you are feeling at the threshold of beginning is not a signal that you are wrong to be here. It is a signal that there is a root to go to. And when you go to that root, what you often find is not confirmation of the fear. You find the belief that was generating it. And you find that the belief, like all beliefs, is not the truth. It is just something that happened once, that your system decided meant something, and that has been quietly making decisions on your behalf ever since.

What I know from that experience, and from watching hundreds of practitioners navigate the same territory since, is this: the imposter syndrome is not evidence that you are not ready. It is evidence that you care. The practitioner who feels no fear at the beginning of this work is either extraordinarily regulated, which takes time and personal healing to build — or not yet fully grasping the weight of what they are being trusted with. The fear means you understand the responsibility. That is not disqualifying. That is appropriate.

The question is not how to make the fear disappear before you begin. The question is whether you are willing to begin while it is still present.

The imposter syndrome is not evidence that you are not ready. It is evidence that you care. The question is not how to make the fear disappear before you begin — it is whether you are willing to begin while it is still present.

— — —

What Imposter Syndrome Is Really Saying

When I work with students who are struggling to take the step from trained to practising, the imposter syndrome almost always reveals itself as a cluster of specific limiting beliefs. They are so consistent across different people, different backgrounds, different levels of prior training, that I have come to think of them as almost universal to this particular transition.

Imposter syndrome is not, at its core, a bad thing. It means you care. It means you have not yet made the mistake of believing you have nothing left to learn. A practitioner with no imposter syndrome at the beginning is a practitioner who has not yet fully reckoned with the weight of what they are being trusted with. The doubt is appropriate. The question is only whether you let it make the decision, or whether you make it instead.

The belief that they need to know more before they are ready. The belief that other practitioners are more qualified, more experienced, more naturally suited to this work. The belief that if a client does not experience a significant shift in session, it will be because of a personal failing rather than simply the nature of any given session on any given day. The belief that charging for this work is somehow presumptuous, that they have not yet earned the right to receive in exchange for what they give.

And underneath all of these, usually: the belief that they are not enough. Which is, of course, a belief we address in every client who sits across from us. And which, in practitioners who have not yet done sufficient work on their own roots, continues to quietly shape every professional decision, who to approach, what to charge, how much to offer, whether to begin at all.

The work is the same work. It applies to the practitioner just as it applies to the client. And the practitioner who has genuinely addressed these roots in their own healing, who knows in their body, not just their mind, that they are enough — will practise from a fundamentally different place than the one who is still running from the wound.

This is why personal healing is not a nice-to-have for RCT practitioners. It is the foundation. Not because you must be finished — nobody is ever finished — but because the degree to which you have cleared your own roots is the degree to which you can be fully present for someone else's.

The Students Who Surprised Me Most

In a decade of training practitioners, the ones who have surprised me most are not the ones with the most prior experience or the most impressive credentials. They are the ones who had done the most of their own work.

A woman who had spent twenty years in corporate accounting, who came to RCT through her own healing journey and who initially seemed, from the outside, the least likely candidate for a healing practice — she was seeing clients within three months of certification and building a waiting list within six months. Not because she had perfect technique. Because she had done enough of her own healing that clients felt genuinely safe in her presence. And genuine safety, as we have explored throughout this book, is the ground from which all healing grows.

A man who had been a schoolteacher for fifteen years and who almost did not complete the training because the imposter syndrome convinced him, at week three, that he did not belong in the room. He stayed. He did the work. He went to the root of the belief that had been telling him for his entire adult life that he was not the kind of person who helped people in this way. What he found there surprised him. What he built afterward surprised him more.

I tell these stories because the people who most doubt their readiness are often the ones most needed in this work. The doubt is not disqualifying. It is information. And like all information that arises in the context of this method, it can be traced to a root, healed at its source, and released — leaving behind someone who can step fully into what they came here to do.

The people who most doubt their readiness are often the ones most needed in this work. The doubt is not disqualifying. It is information. Trace it to its root. Heal it. And step in.

— — —

Beginning Before You Feel Ready

There is a particular quality of waiting that I have observed in new practitioners who do not begin, a waiting that is always for something just out of reach. One more course. One more supervision session. One more year of their own healing work. One more sign from the world that it is the right moment.

The right moment does not arrive before you begin. It arrives through beginning.

Your first sessions will not be your best sessions. They will be the sessions that teach you what no training can teach, the feel of being in the room with real material, the way your own nervous system responds to different presentations, the particular strengths and edges of your own practice. They will be sessions that you will look back on in two years and understand much more than you understood at the time. And they will be sessions that, even in their imperfection, will reach people who needed to be reached.

This is part of what the RCT certification training is designed to support. It has been built as a step-by-step, practical methodology, a clear sequence of what to do next, that works for someone who is brand new to this kind of work and has only their own lived healing experience to draw from, and equally for trained mental health professionals who have been practising for decades. You do not need prior credentials. You need commitment, personal healing, and the willingness to learn. The training includes a community of fellow practitioners and students to practice with as you build your confidence, weekly live calls, and live business and marketing training for running sessions both online and in person. If you would like to experience a session before enrolling, you can find a certified practitioner through the directory at thecentreforhealing.com/practitioner-directory.

Because here is what I know from watching this happen many times: even an imperfect RCT session — one where the practitioner is nervous, where the timing is slightly off, where the questions are not quite as precise as they will later become — contains something that most of the conventional therapeutic world is not offering. It contains the root-cause question. It contains the trust in the unconscious mind as intelligent and capable. It contains the willingness to go where the healing leads rather than where the theory predicts. And that orientation, even in its earliest and most tentative expression, produces results that surprise everyone in the room.

So begin. Begin with the clients who come to you through natural connection — friends, family members, colleagues who have heard what you are doing and who are curious. Begin with a package that feels manageable — three or four sessions, clearly priced, honestly described. Begin with supervision so that you have someone to bring the difficult sessions to, someone who can help you see what you could not see from inside the room. And begin with your own continued healing, because every root you clear in yourself deepens the ground you stand on when you are holding space for someone else.

The world needs practitioners of this work. It needs them badly, and it needs more of them than currently exist. The person reading this book is, in all likelihood, someone who found their way here because something in their own life called them toward healing — their own, and eventually others'. That calling is not accidental. It is not imposter syndrome trying to disguise itself as purpose. It is purpose, with imposter syndrome sitting in the way of it.

— — —

Supporting Clients Between Sessions

One of the qualities that separates RCT from many other therapeutic approaches is what happens in the space between sessions. The work does not pause when the client leaves the room. Healing continues to integrate. Old patterns surface for review. New responses begin to take root. And the client, often for the first time in their life, is navigating this process consciously rather than being carried along by it.

This means that the practitioner's responsibility does not end at the close of a session. It extends, in a thoughtful and boundaried way, into the days that follow. Not because clients need to be managed between sessions, but because a little well-placed support at the right moment can be the difference between integration and overwhelm.

In practice, this might look like: a brief check-in message two or three days after a particularly deep session; a set of grounding practices or affirmations personalised to what was worked on; access to a short audio or resource that supports the specific belief that was addressed; or simply the reassurance that what they are feeling in the days after a session — the tiredness, the emotional surfacing, the strange dreams — is a normal and healthy part of the process. Knowing this in advance prevents clients from interpreting integration as regression.

Many practitioners find it useful to send a short follow-up note after each session — two or three sentences that name what was worked on, affirm the progress made, and remind the client of any practices or awarenesses to carry into the week. This note takes less than five minutes to write and can have a disproportionate impact on how safely and confidently the client holds themselves in the days before you meet again.

The boundary to hold is this: between-session support is offered to support integration, not to extend the therapeutic relationship into an on-call arrangement. Clear expectations set at the beginning of the client journey — about what is available, how to use it, and what warrants reaching out versus waiting for the next scheduled session — protect both the practitioner and the client. Support between sessions is an act of care. It is not the same as being available without limit.

The Centre for Healing provides practitioners with a library of between-session resources, integrative practices, and follow-up templates as part of the RCT certification. These are tools designed to be personalised and offered in the practitioner's own voice — not scripts, but starting points for the ongoing container that makes this work genuinely transformative rather than just therapeutically productive.

— — —

> *"The Root-Cause Therapy certification gave me so much more than just a set of tools. It supported deep personal healing while teaching me how to hold space for others in a safe, structured and powerful way. Melissa's presence throughout the course is warm and real. You can feel the integrity behind everything that's been created."*
>
> — Nelia Joubert-Hartman, RCT Certified Practitioner

Go to the root of the imposter syndrome. And then step through.

— — —

Reflection

> *What is the one thing you have been waiting to feel ready for? And is it possible that the waiting itself is the thing that needs healing?*

Your reflection:

Chapter Twenty-One: Building Your Practice

The Internal Architecture: What You Need to Believe First

There are three beliefs that I have seen block more practitioners from building the practice they are capable of building than any external factor. They are worth naming directly.

The first is the belief that charging for healing work is somehow less ethical than offering it freely. This belief is extraordinarily common, and it has roots in a deep cultural narrative about what spiritual or healing service is supposed to look like — selfless, unboundaried, separate from the world of commerce. The practitioners who carry this belief tend to undercharge dramatically, to give away significant amounts of unpaid time, and to burn out inside two years because the practice is not financially sustainable. The truth is this: a practice that does not sustain the practitioner economically cannot sustain the practitioner at all. And a practitioner who is financially stressed, overworked, and depleted cannot provide the quality of regulated, grounded, genuinely present care that this work requires. Charging appropriately for what you offer is not greed. It is the condition of ongoing service.

The second is the belief that marketing is manipulative, that talking about your work publicly, sharing what you do and what it produces, is somehow incompatible with the integrity of the healing space. This belief keeps practitioners invisible and keeps the people who need this work from finding it. Marketing, for healers, is simply communication — telling the truth about what you do, who it is for, and what becomes possible when someone commits to the process. The person who finds you through your honest, visible presence and makes an informed choice to work with you is not a person you have manipulated. They are a person you have reached.

The third is the belief that results speak for themselves and that a good practitioner should not need to ask for referrals, testimonials, or visibility. Results do speak — but only to the people already in the room. The person who is still searching, who has not yet found their way to this work, cannot hear the results of sessions they have not yet had. You have to go and meet them where they are. That requires visibility. And visibility requires the willingness to be seen before you know how it will be received.

> ***Practitioner Note |*** *If any of these three beliefs resonates as something you carry, take it to the sway. Test it. Find its root. The limiting belief that is keeping your practice small has an origin, just like every other limiting belief your clients bring. Heal it at the source, and watch what becomes possible in your professional life.*

— — —

The Client Journey: From First Contact to Lasting Change

A thriving RCT practice is built on a clear, consistent, and genuinely caring client journey, the sequence of experiences a person moves through from the moment they first encounter you to the point where they complete their work with you and carry what they have built forward into their life.

It begins before the first session. It begins with how you present your work in the world, the language you use, the stories you share, the clarity with which you describe what RCT is and what it is not. People considering this work are often carrying years of failed attempts at other approaches, and they are weighing the cost of hoping again. The way you describe what you do either speaks to their actual experience or it does not. Speak to it directly. Speak to the pattern that persists despite everything they have already tried. Speak to the exhaustion of understanding without change. And speak with the quiet confidence of someone who has seen what this work actually does.

The initial consultation — free, and I recommend keeping it that way — is not a sales conversation. It is a discernment conversation. You are listening to understand whether this person is a good fit for RCT at this moment in their life, whether they are ready for the kind of work this requires, and whether you are the right practitioner for them. They are doing the same. The consultation that ends with both parties feeling genuinely clear — either a confident yes or an honest acknowledgement that this is not the right fit right now — is the one that produces the best outcomes for everyone.

The first session sets the foundation. It is longer than subsequent sessions, the intake form review, the history conversation, the full Testing Sheet run-through, the first Timeline experience. It is also the session in which the therapeutic relationship is established, and that relationship matters as much as anything technical that happens within it. A client who trusts you, who feels genuinely safe in the room with you, who senses that you see them as a whole person rather than a presenting problem, that client will go further in the healing work than one who carries reservations about the relationship, however skilled the technique.

The programme arc — typically eight to twelve sessions, as we explored in Chapter Twelve — is the container in which the deepest and most lasting work happens. Within that arc, each session builds on the previous one, the Testing Sheet tracks the movement of beliefs and emotions over time, and the cumulative picture of healing becomes visible in ways that a single session never could. I recommend presenting RCT to new clients as a programme rather than individual sessions, for this reason. The person who commits to the arc gets qualitatively different results from the person who comes once or twice and then makes a decision based on incomplete evidence.

> ***Practitioner Note |*** *When a client tells you they only want to try one session first, honour that, and also be*

> *honest about what one session can and cannot do. It can give them a genuine experience of the work and a real sense of whether it is for them. It cannot address the layered, cumulative healing that produces lasting change. Give them the one session with full commitment, and at the end, be direct: here is what I think would be possible if we did this properly, across a full programme. Let them make an informed choice.*

— — —

Packaging and Pricing: What Sustainability Looks Like

The most common pricing mistake I see new practitioners make is charging by the hour for individual sessions. This creates a practice model that is financially fragile, clinically suboptimal, and practically unsustainable. It is fragile because income is entirely dependent on session-by-session booking, with no security between. It is clinically suboptimal because clients who are paying session by session tend to drop off when the work becomes difficult rather than staying through the passage that precedes significant change. And it is unsustainable because the hourly rate required to build a genuinely viable income from individual sessions is typically higher than new practitioners feel comfortable charging.

The alternative is programme-based packaging. A programme, a clearly defined number of sessions, offered as a complete investment, paid upfront or across an agreed schedule — solves all three problems simultaneously. It provides income security. It creates client commitment through the difficult passages. And it allows a price point that reflects the genuine value of the arc of work rather than the hourly rate of any individual session. It also creates a safe container for them to receive your support, during integration, in-between sessions.

What should a programme cost? This question has no universal answer, because it depends on your location, your market, your experience level, and the specific client population you are serving. It is also worth checking in with your nervous system. If a price feels like too much to say out loud — if quoting it makes you want to apologise or immediately offer a discount, that is information. Either the price needs to come down until you can hold it with confidence, or there is belief work to do around your own worth and what you offer. What I can tell you is that the number should be arrived at not by calculating what you think people will tolerate, but by calculating what you need to earn per client to sustain a practice that is genuinely good — one where you are not overloaded, where you have time for your own ongoing healing and supervision, where the quality of your presence in sessions is not compromised by financial stress. Price from that calculation, and then test whether the market supports it. Most practitioners discover that it does because the people who are genuinely ready for this work understand that genuine, root-level change is worth a genuine investment.

Price from what you need to sustain a practice that is genuinely good — not from what you fear people will say yes to. Most practitioners discover that the people ready for this work understand its value.

— — —

Marketing for Healers: Being Found by the Right People

Marketing for healing practitioners is most effective when it is built on one principle: speak honestly about real transformation. Not abstract promises. Not clinical language that nobody outside the field understands. The real experience of what changes when someone does this work — told in the language of the people who need it, which is the language of the patterns they are exhausted by and the life they are aching toward.

The most powerful marketing available to an RCT practitioner is a genuine testimonial from a client who has been genuinely changed. When someone who has lived the pattern, tried other approaches, and found a different outcome through this work describes that experience in their own words, that reaches people that no crafted marketing message can reach. Collect these. Protect your clients' privacy carefully and completely, but where clients are willing and have given informed consent, their words are the most authentic advertisement your practice has.

Social media, used well, is an extension of the same principle. Sharing educational content that helps potential clients understand what is keeping them stuck, the way beliefs form, why emotions stay stored in the body, how the self-fulfilling prophecy of relationship patterns works — builds trust, demonstrates genuine expertise, and reaches people who would never find you through a directory listing or a search engine. You are not broadcasting at your audience. You are thinking aloud, in public, about things that matter to the people who need what you offer.

In-person connection, referrals, and professional relationships with complementary practitioners — GPs, psychologists, physiotherapists, osteopaths, yoga teachers, breathwork facilitators — are among the most reliable sources of new clients for an established practice. These relationships take time to build, and they are built through genuine connection and mutual respect rather than transactional referral arrangements. Show up. Be present in the communities where the people you serve already are. Let the work speak when people ask about it, without overselling or underselling. And let the relationships form naturally, as all good relationships do.

Sustaining Yourself in the Work

A final word that belongs in any honest chapter about building a healing practice, because it is the thing practitioners most rarely attend to until the consequences become impossible to ignore.

This work is extraordinary. It is also demanding — in ways that are different from most other forms of demanding work, because the demands are not primarily intellectual or physical. They are relational and energetic. Sitting with the depth of another person's pain, holding the container of their healing session after session, carrying the weight of genuine care for each client's progress. This asks something of the practitioner's nervous system that accumulates over time if it is not consciously tended.

Supervision is not optional. It is the professional and ethical minimum, and beyond that, it is the single most effective tool available for maintaining the quality of your own presence in the room. Bring your difficult sessions. Bring the clients you are not sure how to help. Bring the moments when something in you contracted or avoided or was not as present as it needed to be. The supervision relationship is where your own professional growing edge lives, and attending to it consistently is what makes a practice sustainable over the long term.

Your own continued healing work is equally non-negotiable. Not because you must be finished — nobody is ever finished — but because the material that your clients bring will inevitably activate material of your own. If that material is unaddressed, it will find its way into the room. If it is attended to, it deepens the ground from which you work. Every RCT practitioner I know who has built a lasting practice is someone who is genuinely, continuously doing their own work. Not as performance or professional obligation. As lived commitment to the same process they are inviting their clients into.

— — —

Reflection

> *What beliefs do you carry about being seen, about charging for your gifts, or about whether you are 'qualified enough' to help others? Where do you think those beliefs came from?*

Your reflection:

— — —

Chapter Twenty-Two: Your Global Impact

That vision is ambitious. It is also, I believe, possible. And the practitioners trained in this method are the people making it real.

What One Healed Person Changes

When a person heals their root wounds, the effect does not stay contained to them. We explored this in the chapter on generational trauma, the research showing that what is healed in one generation does not get passed to the next. But the ripple extends further than the family line.

A person who has healed their belief that they are not enough shows up differently in every relationship they are part of. They parent differently. They partner differently. They lead differently in their workplace. They are more capable of genuine kindness because they are no longer running from scarcity. They are less likely to harm others unconsciously, because the wound that was driving unconscious harm has been addressed. They have more capacity for the kind of genuine presence that every human being in their orbit benefits from.

Multiply that by every client who passes through an RCT practitioner's practice. Multiply it by every practitioner trained. Multiply it by the families and communities and workplaces and schools those practitioners and their clients inhabit. The mathematics of healing, when it reaches its roots rather than just managing its surface, is extraordinary.

This is not hyperbole. It is what the science of epigenetics is beginning to confirm, that healing is transmissible across generations, just as trauma is. And it is what I have observed, in the most ordinary and most profound terms, across a decade of this work: people who heal change the world around them without trying. Simply by becoming more themselves.

People who heal change the world around them without trying. Simply by becoming more themselves.

I think of it like dropping a stone into still water. The point of contact is a single person — one client, one session, one root healed. But the effect does not stay there. The rings move outward. A parent who heals their wound around worth shows up differently with their children — not performing patience, but genuinely present in a way they could not access before. A partner who heals their fear of abandonment stops creating the very distance they were terrified of. A person who heals their belief that they are not enough stops punishing the people around them for failing to prove otherwise. Each of these shifts reaches everyone in that person's life — often without a word being spoken about healing, or RCT, or any of this. Simply through the change in how they are.

The rings keep moving. The children of that parent carry something different into their own relationships. The partner who felt the shift becomes slightly more able to offer it in turn. The colleague, the friend, the stranger in the shop who simply encountered someone who was genuinely at peace rather than managing a wound — they all carry a trace of it. This is not poetic exaggeration. It is how nervous systems actually work. We are profoundly, biologically attuned to each other. Regulation is contagious. Healing — real healing — spreads.

There is one more image I want to leave you with, because I think it captures something essential about why the quality of your own healing matters so much to the quality of your practice. Think of your mind as a battery — with a finite charge at any given time. When a battery is running many functions simultaneously, the charge disperses and depletes quickly. The more internal conflicts we carry, the more beliefs still running in the background, the more unresolved pain still drawing on the system's resources, the more our energy is fragmented rather than focused. We show up to sessions giving what is left after everything else has taken its share.

But a battery directing its charge toward a single task is a different thing entirely. Focused energy. Full presence. The quality of attention that a practitioner brings when they are not divided, when they are not managing their own anxiety about whether they are enough, not triggered by the client's material because it mirrors their own unhealed wound, not depleted by beliefs that have been quietly running since childhood, that quality of attention is the most powerful therapeutic instrument available. It is not a technique. It is what you become through your own healing work.

Every root you heal in yourself is an investment in every client you will ever sit with. Every belief you clear is one less thing drawing charge away from your presence. This is why we say that personal healing is not a nice-to-have for RCT practitioners — it is the foundation of the work. Not because you must be finished. Nobody is ever finished. But because the degree to which you have cleared your own roots is the degree to which you can be fully there for someone else's.

— — —

The COVID Chapter: When Everything Moved Online

There is a story from the early years of the pandemic that I want to include here, because it illustrates something important about the reach of this work and about what becomes possible when necessity forces innovation.

When the lockdowns began in Melbourne in 2020, Ryan and I had just had our baby and were in the process of relocating — we ended up on a tropical island during a period when almost everything in the conventional world had ground to a halt. The Centre for Healing, which had operated as a physical outpatient clinic, had to make a decision: stop, or find a way to continue.

We moved everything online. Not as a compromise or a stopgap, but as a genuine reconfiguration of how the work could be delivered. And what we discovered — what practitioners across the world who made the same move discovered simultaneously — was that the core of this work does not require physical presence. The Timeline is not in the room. The unconscious mind does not need to be in the same building as the practitioner. The healing that happens in a Zoom session, when both parties are properly prepared and genuinely present, is the same healing that happens in person.

This matters for the vision. Because a method that can be delivered online is a method that can reach anywhere in the world with an internet connection. The practitioner in rural New South Wales can work with a client in Norway. The practitioner in South Africa can serve a client in Canada. The geographical barriers that have always limited the reach of high-quality therapeutic support, the barriers that have meant that root-cause healing was available only to people who could travel to specific cities or afford specific practitioners — are substantially dissolved by a method that works as well at a distance as it does in person.

The RCT practitioners currently working online are building something that has never existed before at this scale: a genuinely global healing community, connected by a shared method and a shared commitment, able to reach people wherever they are in the world and whatever their local access to conventional therapeutic resources might be.

— — —

— — —

A Practice Without Borders

One of the most significant and underappreciated aspects of RCT as a professional pathway is this: it is not bound by the regulatory frameworks that govern registered clinical professions in most countries. Root-Cause Therapy is practised as a complementary and alternative modality, not as a government-registered psychological or counselling profession. This distinction has profound practical implications for how and where practitioners can work.

A licensed psychologist or registered counsellor in Australia must practise within the regulatory requirements of AHPRA. A therapist registered in the UK operates under BACP or UKCP guidelines. Their ability to work with clients in other countries is subject to complex and often restrictive jurisdictional requirements. An RCT practitioner faces none of these barriers. Accredited through the IICT, IAOTH and ICAHP — internationally recognised bodies for complementary therapy — an RCT practitioner in Melbourne can legally and ethically work with a client in Norway, the United States, South Africa, or anywhere else in the world with an internet connection.

This is not a loophole. It is the legitimate and intentional space in which complementary and alternative therapies operate globally. The client is not receiving a government-registered clinical service. They are receiving a deeply skilled, trauma-informed, root-cause healing service from a practitioner who has been rigorously trained and internationally accredited in that specific modality. For many clients, particularly those who have found limited benefit from conventional approaches, the distinction is not a concern at all. It is simply how they access the help they have been looking for.

In practical terms, this means that the world is your client base. A practitioner who builds an online RCT practice is not limited by geography, by the size of their local market, or by the regulatory boundaries of their home country. They can reach the person in rural Iceland who has never had access to trauma-informed support. The executive in Singapore who cannot risk being seen entering a psychologist's office. The mother in Brazil who found a practitioner's Instagram and felt, for the first time, that someone understood what she was carrying.

This is part of what makes the global reach of RCT not just an aspiration but an achievable reality for individual practitioners. You do not need a bricks-and-mortar clinic. You do not need to be registered in every country you serve. You need a trained skill set, a quality online setup, and the willingness to show up fully for whoever finds their way to you — wherever they are in the world.

— — —

What the World Is Asking For

We are living through a period of collective reckoning with mental health on a scale that previous generations had no framework for. The data is not ambiguous: anxiety, depression, trauma, addiction, and the social and relational damage that flows from unhealed wounds are among the most significant challenges facing every society on the planet. The conventional mental health system, even at its most resourced, is not keeping pace with the scale of what is needed. Waiting lists are long. Evidence-based approaches are effective for some presentations and largely ineffective for others. And the root-cause question, the question that asks not just what is happening but why, and what needs to heal for it to change — is still asked remarkably rarely in conventional settings.

The people training in RCT and building practices from this foundation are part of the answer to that gap. Not the only answer — no single method or community is — but a genuine, meaningful, root-cause contribution to one of the most important questions of our time.

That is the context in which your practice exists. Not just a business. Not just a career. A contribution. And the quality of that contribution, the depth of your own healing, the regulatedness of your presence, the precision and care of your clinical work — is directly proportional to the number of lives you will genuinely touch.

What I Want to Leave You With

This book began with a question: what if the pattern is not the problem? What if it is the answer, the nervous system's intelligent response to something that has never been given the space to heal?

Everything that has followed has been an attempt to answer that question in depth, the science, the framework, the method, the specific protocols for specific presentations, the personal stories of what healing looks like from the inside. All of it pointing toward the same understanding: that the human system is not broken. It is responding. And when we find what it is responding to, and we heal that at its source, the response no longer needs to be what it was.

I want to leave you with something that goes beyond technique. It is the orientation that underlies everything in this book and everything in the training.

The client who sits across from you is not their presenting problem. They are not their diagnosis, their pattern, their history of failed attempts, their current level of suffering. They are the whole, intact, extraordinary person who has been faithfully doing the best they could with what they were given, and who has found their way, through whatever path brought them here, to a room where someone is finally going to ask the question that changes everything.

What happened? And what needs to heal so that it no longer has to run your life from underneath?

That question, asked with genuine care and genuine skill in a genuinely safe space, is the foundation of all healing work. The method provides the structure. The protocols provide the precision. The science provides the understanding. But the question, and the quality of presence from which it is asked — is the beginning of everything.

The client who sits across from you is not their presenting problem. They are the whole, intact person who has been faithfully doing the best they could with what they were given, and who has found their way to someone who will finally ask the question that changes everything.

— — —

Thank you for reading this book. Thank you for the healing you have done in your own life that brought you to the point of wanting to offer this to others. Thank you for what you are about to build, the sessions you are about to sit in, the roots you are about to help heal, the generational chains you are about to help break.

The world is asking for this. You are the answer it is looking for.

Now begin.

What Practitioners Are Saying

The following are reviews from practitioners and students who have trained in Root-Cause Therapy through The Centre for Healing. They are shared here in their own words.

> *"I love the concept of root cause therapy. The connection one develops with Self on all levels is simply transformative for clients and practitioners alike. Mel is supportive, patient, and passionate about sharing this incredible modality with the world."*
>
> — Ira Jowett, RCT Certified Practitioner ★★★★★

> *"Having already gained RCT certification, which is a game-changer, I was excited to embark on the Trauma Informed Manifestation Certification. It did not disappoint! I pretty much felt the effects almost immediately. This is truly incredible work."*
>
> — Pamela Kay, RCT Certified Practitioner ★★★★★

> *"I took the Root Cause Therapy training and the content was so good, full of insightful information, easy to understand, well structured. It's also a beautiful community. I loved doing sessions with my peers. Absolutely recommend."*

— Alexiane, RCT Certified Practitioner ★★★★★

"I'm a member of the Healing Hub and have completed Level 1 and 2 of the Root Cause Therapy programme. I loved the course and love how it's chunked up into manageable sections. Level 2 totally blew my mind. The work we are doing on ourselves as practitioners is invaluable."

— Miss Walton, RCT Practitioner ★★★★★

"First, the modality I trained in is absolutely amazing and empowering, whether experiencing it or leading a session! Second, the community and support is so abundant! The resources have continued to add so much value to my ongoing development as a practitioner."

— Sara Early, RCT Certified Practitioner ★★★★★

"This training has been by far the most outstanding course I have ever completed. Not only has it helped me understand myself on a deeper level, but I have already started to see changes in my clients in the short time since qualifying."

— Alison Walters, RCT Certified Practitioner ★★★★★

"The Root Cause Therapy program covers everything you need to know in a clear and

engaging way. I truly appreciate how generously they share what has worked for them. Wonderful programs, wonderful people, an organisation I highly recommend."

— Ilona, RCT Certified Practitioner ★★★★★

"Studying RCT has changed my life. I am proud to be a student, practitioner, and member of this community. I'm not stopping here — I have three more courses with The Centre for Healing to complete, and will no doubt continue beyond that."

— Siobhan, RCT Certified Practitioner ★★★★★

"The Centre for Healing is a haven of grounded and effective somatic training and community. World class."

— Alena Turley, RCT Certified Practitioner ★★★★★

— — —

If you feel called to this work, whether you are a complete beginner or an experienced practitioner looking for a deeper method — you can find out more about the RCT certification training at thecentreforhealing.com

To experience a session with a certified RCT practitioner before enrolling, visit the practitioner directory at thecentreforhealing.com/practitioner-directory

Take the Next Step

Root-Cause Therapy has the power to change lives — yours, and those of everyone you work with. Here is how to go deeper with The Centre for Healing community.

Watch the free introduction training and see the method in action:

thecentreforhealing.com/webinar-registration

Enrol in the RCT Certification Course and begin your practitioner journey:

https://www.thecentreforhealing.com/root-cause-therapy-certification-1

Explore our full library of courses, free resources, blog, podcast, and app, and join one of the warmest healing communities anywhere in the world:

thecentreforhealing.com

— — —

Also by Melissa Hiemann:

The Natural High — Secrets to Overcoming Instant Gratification and Finding Inner Peace

— — —

The world needs practitioners of this work. It needs more of them than currently exist. You are the answer it is looking for. Now begin.

References

The following works are cited or drawn upon throughout this book.

— — —

1. Felitti, V. J., Anda, R. F., Nordenberg, D., Williamson, D. F., Spitz, A. M., Edwards, V., Koss, M. P., & Marks, J. S. (1998). Relationship of childhood abuse and household dysfunction to many of the leading causes of death in adults: The Adverse Childhood Experiences (ACE) Study. American Journal of Preventive Medicine, 14(4), 245–258.

2. Felitti, V. J. (2003). The origins of addiction: Evidence from the Adverse Childhood Experiences Study. Praxis der Kinderpsychologie und Kinderpsychiatrie, 51(6), 547–559.

3. Goodheart, G. J. (1964–1966). Applied Kinesiology: Research Manuals. Detroit: Privately published.

4. Bowlby, J. (1969). Attachment and Loss, Vol. 1: Attachment. New York: Basic Books.

5. Lipton, B. H. (2005). The Biology of Belief: Unleashing the Power of Consciousness, Matter & Miracles. Carlsbad, CA: Hay House.

6. Hawkins, D. R. (1995). Power vs. Force: The Hidden Determinants of Human Behavior. Carlsbad, CA: Hay House.

7. Church, D. (2007). The Genie in Your Genes: Epigenetic Medicine and the New Biology of Intention. Santa Rosa, CA: Energy Psychology Press.

8. Dias, B. G., & Ressler, K. J. (2014). Parental olfactory experience influences behavior and neural structure in subsequent generations. Nature Neuroscience, 17(1), 89–96.

9. Bandler, R., & Grinder, J. (1979). Frogs into Princes: Neuro Linguistic Programming. Moab, UT: Real People Press.

10. Chamberlain, D. (1998). The Mind of Your Newborn Baby. Berkeley, CA: North Atlantic Books.

11. Verny, T., & Kelly, J. (1981). The Secret Life of the Unborn Child. New York: Summit Books.

12. Levine, P. A. (1997). Waking the Tiger: Healing Trauma. Berkeley, CA: North Atlantic Books.

13. Levine, P. A. (2010). In an Unspoken Voice: How the Body Releases Trauma and Restores Goodness. Berkeley, CA: North Atlantic Books.

14. James, T., & Woodsmall, W. (1988). Time Line Therapy and the Basis of Personality. Capitola, CA: Meta Publications.

15. Maté, G. (2008). In the Realm of Hungry Ghosts: Close Encounters with Addiction. Toronto: Knopf Canada.

16. Maté, G. (2022). The Myth of Normal: Trauma, Illness, and Healing in a Toxic Culture. New York: Avery.

17. van der Kolk, B. (2014). The Body Keeps the Score: Brain, Mind, and Body in the Healing of Trauma. New York: Viking.

18. Jung, C. G. (1953–1979). The Collected Works of C. G. Jung. Princeton, NJ: Princeton University Press.

Glossary

Key terms used in Root-Cause Therapy

— — —

Calibration

The process of establishing a reliable baseline response with the sway test at the start of a session. The practitioner asks the client to test a known true statement (their own name) and a known false statement to confirm the body's response is clear and consistent before beginning belief work.

Client Feedback Ratings

A section of the Testing Sheet where the client rates areas of their life on a scale of one to ten at the start of each session. Ratings track subjective experience across domains such as stress, anxiety, relationships, and energy, creating a visible record of change over time.

Dissociation

A nervous system response in which a person becomes disconnected from their thoughts, feelings, body, or surroundings, often as a protective response to overwhelming experience. In RCT sessions, the practitioner watches for signs of dissociation and has specific protocols for gently re-grounding the client.

Extended Testing Sheet

An addition to the Level 1 Testing Sheet that includes additional domains such as relationships, money blocks, and specific physical issues. Used once the foundational belief work of the Level 1 sheet is substantially complete.

Future Session

Usually done at the closing stage of an RCT program, in which the client travels forward along their Timeline to a point in the future, experiencing themselves living with the newly integrated belief, where their current issues are resolved. This anchors the healing in the body and the unconscious as a felt sense reality, not just a cognitive understanding.

Genealogical Trauma

Emotional, physical, or behavioural patterns inherited through family lineage rather than directly experienced (through maternal and paternal DNA). Supported by epigenetic research showing that traumatic experiences can alter gene expression in ways that are passed across generations. RCT includes specific processes for identifying and resolving genealogical material.

Higher Self

The aspect of a person's consciousness that holds wisdom, perspective, and compassion beyond the conditioned self. In RCT Timeline work, the practitioner may invite the client's Higher Self/ Soul to be present during healing processes, particularly when working with younger parts of the self.

Inner Child

The part of a person's unconscious that holds memories, emotions, and beliefs formed in childhood. In RCT, inner child healing involves returning to the original event where a belief formed, providing the younger self with the understanding, safety, or love that was absent at the time.

Intake Form

A detailed questionnaire completed by the client before their first session. The practitioner uses this information to pre-fill the Testing Sheet with likely beliefs and patterns, arriving at the first session already oriented to the client's history and presenting concerns.

Level 1 Testing Sheet

The foundational Testing Sheet containing the core emotions, limiting beliefs, and life domain ratings used in standard RCT sessions. Typically the primary working document for the first eight to twelve sessions of a client's healing journey.

Limiting Belief

An unconscious conclusion about the self or the world formed in response to a painful or overwhelming experience, most commonly in childhood. Examples include 'I am not enough,' 'I am not safe,' and 'I am not loved.' In RCT, limiting beliefs are identified through sway testing and resolved at their root through Timeline healing.

Monitor

A section of the Testing Sheet used to track specific thoughts, behaviours, or patterns the client is watching during the week between sessions. Monitoring creates awareness and provides data for the following session.

Muscle Testing

Also known as applied kinesiology, a method of accessing the body's unconscious responses through subtle physical feedback. In RCT, the primary form of muscle testing is the Sway Test.

Natal Trauma

Emotional or physical experiences occurring during the birth process or in the early days of life outside the womb. RCT recognises that the nervous system is active and impressionable from birth and that experiences at this stage can form significant beliefs and somatic patterns.

Reparenting

A process within Timeline healing in which the practitioner, or the client's own Higher Self, provides a younger part of the client with the care, attunement, safety, or validation that was absent during the original painful experience. Reparenting does not rewrite history; it provides a new emotional experience that the nervous system can integrate.

Root Cause

The original experience in which a limiting belief, emotional pattern, or somatic response was formed. RCT holds that lasting healing requires addressing the root cause rather than managing its symptoms. The root cause is identified through the Timeline process.

Root-Cause Therapy (RCT)

A trauma-informed, somatic, root-cause healing methodology developed by Melissa Hiemann and Ryan Hassan at The Centre for Healing. RCT integrates Neuro-Linguistic Programming (NLP), hypnotherapy, timeline therapy, somatic awareness, epigenetics, and inner child healing into a structured, repeatable process that addresses limiting beliefs and unresolved emotional experiences at their origin.

Somatic

Relating to the body as distinct from the mind. Somatic awareness in RCT refers to the practitioner's and client's attention to physical sensations, tension, breath, and other body-based signals during sessions, which often indicate where unprocessed material is held.

Sway Test

The primary muscle testing method used in RCT, in which the client stands and observes the body's natural forward or backward sway in response to a stated belief or question. A forward sway indicates a true or aligned response; a backward sway indicates false or misaligned. The sway communicates what the unconscious knows independently of the conscious mind.

Testing Sheet

The single-page diagnostic and session-mapping tool at the centre of RCT practice. It contains the client's header information, life domain feedback ratings, emotions, limiting beliefs, physical symptoms, and monitoring notes. A new Testing Sheet is completed each session, creating a cumulative record of the client's healing journey.

Timeline

The unconscious structure through which people organise their experience of time, typically running from past to future at a consistent angle and direction unique to each person. In RCT, the practitioner guides the client to travel along their Timeline to the root cause of a belief or pattern, facilitating healing at the point of origin.

Timeline Healing

The core healing process in RCT in which the client, in a relaxed and resourced state, travels back along their Timeline to the original event where a belief was formed, receives healing and reparenting at that point, extracts the learning the event carries, and returns to the present with the belief updated.

Unconscious Mind (UCM)

The part of the mind operating below conscious awareness that stores emotional memories, learned patterns, automatic responses, and the beliefs formed from experience. In RCT, the unconscious is treated as an ally with access to information the conscious mind cannot directly reach. The Sway Test and Timeline process both engage the unconscious directly.

Womb Material

Experiences, emotions, or beliefs originating during gestation, in the period before birth. RCT recognises that the developing nervous system absorbs the emotional environment of the mother and that significant material from this period can contribute to patterns that surface in adult life.

Autonomic Nervous System (ANS)

The part of the nervous system that regulates involuntary body functions including heart rate, breathing, digestion, and stress responses. The ANS operates largely outside conscious awareness and underpins the body's survival responses. In RCT, understanding the ANS helps explain why healing must happen at the body level, not just the cognitive level.

Co-Regulation

The neurobiological process by which one person's regulated nervous system helps to calm and stabilise another's. Co-regulation is the foundation of early attachment. In RCT sessions, the practitioner's calm, ventral vagal presence actively supports the client's nervous system to feel safe enough to access and heal stored material.

Dorsal Vagal State

A branch of the parasympathetic nervous system associated with shutdown, collapse, numbness, and dissociation. When the sympathetic fight or flight response has been overwhelmed, the nervous system defaults to dorsal vagal freeze as a last line of defence. Common experiences include depression, disconnection, hopelessness, and feeling physically shut down.

Nervous System Regulation

The capacity to move fluidly between activation and calm, responding appropriately to stress and returning to baseline without becoming stuck. Regulation is not the absence of emotion but the ability to process experience without being overwhelmed by it. RCT builds regulation by resolving the stored experiences that keep the nervous system locked in threat responses.

Neuroception

A term coined by Dr Stephen Porges to describe the nervous system's subconscious process of scanning for safety or danger in the environment. Unlike perception, neuroception happens below the level of thought. Faulty neuroception, often resulting from early trauma, can cause the nervous system to perceive threat where none exists, keeping a person chronically activated or shut down.

Polyvagal Theory

A framework developed by Dr Stephen Porges describing how the autonomic nervous system responds to perceived safety and threat through three hierarchical states: ventral vagal (social engagement and safety), sympathetic (fight or flight), and dorsal vagal (freeze or collapse). Polyvagal

Theory explains why the body must experience safety before lasting change is possible.

Sympathetic Nervous System State

The branch of the autonomic nervous system responsible for mobilising the body in response to perceived threat, commonly known as fight or flight. When activated, the sympathetic state increases heart rate, releases adrenaline and cortisol, and prepares the body for action. In unresolved trauma, this state can become chronically activated, manifesting as anxiety, anger, and hypervigilance.

Trauma Response

The nervous system's automatic, protective reaction to an experience perceived as overwhelming or life-threatening. Trauma responses including fight, flight, freeze, and fawn are not character flaws but intelligent survival adaptations. They become problematic when the nervous system remains stuck in a response long after the original threat has passed.

Ventral Vagal State

The highest-order branch of the parasympathetic nervous system, associated with social engagement, connection, curiosity, and felt safety. When in a ventral vagal state, a person can connect with others, think clearly, and experience genuine rest. This is the state that RCT works toward as a natural outcome of resolving stored experiences that have kept the system in lower states of defence.

About the Author

Melissa Hiemann knows what it is to need healing before knowing how to find it. Her own path through addiction, trauma, and a nervous system that had learned to brace rather than trust is the foundation beneath everything she has built. It is why the work is what it is — not assembled from theory, but developed in the lived reality of what actually helps people change.

She is the creator of Root-Cause Therapy and the co-founder of The Centre for Healing, which she built with her partner Ryan Hassan in 2016. What began as a small practice has grown into a global training organisation, certifying practitioners across more than thirty countries in trauma-informed, somatic, root-cause methods. The Centre is internationally accredited with the IICT, ICAHP and IAOTH. Along with offering CPD's for certain industries.

Her work draws together Neuro-Linguistic Programming (NLP), hypnotherapy, timeline therapy, somatic practice, and epigenetics into a single cohesive framework that addresses not just symptoms, but the origin of patterns. She has worked with thousands of clients and trained hundreds of practitioners, and continues to develop the RCT methodology through ongoing clinical work and research.

She is also the author of *The Natural High: Secrets to Overcoming Instant Gratification and Finding Inner Peace*, which shares the personal story that preceded this work and the understanding she arrived at about why we reach for what we reach for.

Melissa lives with her family in Australia and continues to train practitioners, see clients, and ask the same question that started all of this: what is actually underneath this pattern, and what does it need in order to finally heal?

Find Melissa and The Centre for Healing

thecentreforhealing.com

instagram.com/thecentreforhealing

youtube.com/@thecentreforhealing

To train in Root-Cause Therapy and join the global practitioner community, visit thecentreforhealing.com

www.ingramcontent.com/pod-product-compliance
Ingram Content Group UK Ltd.
Pitfield, Milton Keynes, MK11 3LW, UK
UKHW060007051026
15591UKWH00001B/81
* 9 7 8 0 6 4 8 9 4 6 0 2 1 *